A PERSONAL GUIDE TO PERSONAL COMPUTING

A PERSONAL GUIDE TO PERSONAL COMPUTING

Geof Wheelwright

Quiller Press
London

First published in 1987 by

Quiller Press Ltd
50 Albemarle Street
London W1X 4BD

ISBN 0 907621 81 3

Design by Tina Dutton and Kate Hughes-Stanton;
design and production in association with
Book Production Consultants, Cambridge

Typeset by Goodfellow & Egan, Cambridge

Printed in Great Britain
at the University Printing House, Oxford
by David Stanford
Printer to the University

Front cover illustration of an Intel 80386 computer
processor chip courtesy of Intel Corp.

FOR YVETTE

without whom I would not have
had the support and inspiration to
complete this opus. Thanks also to
John and all at A Plus for their
patience and understanding – and
finally to Compaq for its backing
and technical assistance.

CONTENTS

PART III Making the most of your applications

PREFACE

by Joe McNally,
Managing Director,
Compaq Computer Ltd

Innovation and standardisation have always been the keys to our success at Compaq. When we designed our first machines – the Compaq Portable and Compaq Deskpro – we took the hardware standard which had become accepted by business and industry and brought innovation to that standard by adding portability and superior performance.

In agreeing to sponsor the writing, development and research of this book about business applications, we have striven to add further value to the kind of service for which Compaq has become known. There are existing books about using MS–DOS – or simply summarising the types of applications you can buy for your PC. That, if you like, is the 'industry standard'.

Where we have introduced innovation in this case is in using an approach which adds value to the discussion of applications by relating them to the way in which you run your office, by telling you what to look for when you use and choose software and by providing a comprehensive collection of appendices which should serve as a reference document for a long time to come.

The author of this book is also something of an innovative choice. Instead of using one of the many technical writers and engineers who usually write books about computer applications – and discuss them in a somewhat dry and uninteresting manner – we asked experienced author and journalist Geof Wheelwright to take on the job.

As a writer for publications such as *The Times*, *Newsweek* and *PC Magazine* (as well as the author of eight books about computer applications for Pan, Macmillan and Longman), we felt that Geof Wheelwright would be able to provide us with an entertaining read – as well as a thoroughly-researched document which dealt with computer applications from the user's point of view.

The result is a book which we believe is one of the easiest-to-read and most comprehensive guides you are likely to find on the subject of general business applications. It is written by someone experienced in the business of explaining complex concepts in simple terms – and who isn't so caught up in the technicalities of hardware and software design that he loses sight of what you, the user, have to go through.

In short, we are happy to present this *Personal Guide to Personal Computing* as we believe it enhances and adds to the value of our PC range – and hopefully adds to the value you will get out of it.

March 1987

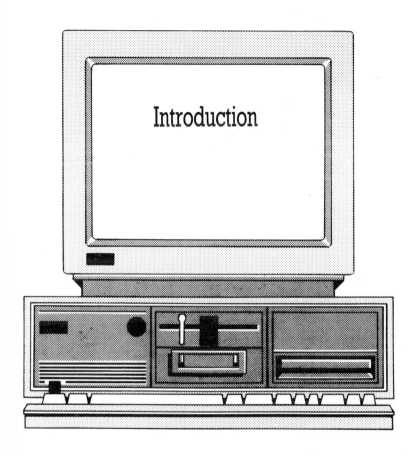

Introduction

The Personal Computer has come of age. At one time, the desktop micro was seen merely as a somewhat quirky adjunct to the large room-filling mainframe and minicomputer systems which populated the MIS and DP departments of the world's major corporations. It is the PC, however, which is now leading the office computer revolution.

Large systems – and large systems houses such as IBM – were expected from the beginning to drive the computerisation of the office. But the predictions were only half-right. Indeed it was IBM that proved to be the leader in the office automation business – but not with the PROFS office automation it originally set up to work

3

with the IBM DISOSS (Distributed Office Architecture) originally developed for mainframe and mini-computers.

It was actually IBM's new Personal Computer system which gave the company its big win in the office market – setting up what many companies call the 'PC phenomenon' which has swept the Western business world. According to the *Financial Times*, PC design proved so popular that IBM's share of the business microcomputer market went from zero in early 1981 to more than 40 per cent by late 1984.

According to estimates by Future Computing, the popularity of IBM's PC fuelled a massive growth in the market in the early 1980s. In 1983 Future found that only 8 per cent (some 4.3 million people) of all office workers in the US were using PCs as a part of their regular work – but that had jumped to between 18 to 20 per cent by 1985, with more than 10 million US workers using micros.

THE FLEXIBLE PC

This massive vote of enthusiasm for the PC was a sign that users were tired of the constraints and limitations of large systems, liked the flexibility and freedom offered by having their own desktop machine which would run their own 'local' software and felt confident buying an IBM-designed product.

It might have all stopped there if IBM had kept its PC 'locked up' and prohibited other manufacturers from releasing hardware and software to run with it. Fortunately, however, Big Blue decided to take the risk of offering an 'open-architecture' computer for which it would provide support and encouragement. This decision – perhaps more than any other – accelerated the popularity of the PC by creating a competitive business in which hundreds of companies were moving very quickly to offer software and hardware support for the machine.

Compaq was one of the first companies to realise this and to recognise that, if it was to succeed in the business PC market, it would have to innovate 'around' the PC standard. Compaq machines would start with PC compatibility as the base feature and built-in additional functionality on top of the compatible base.

The wisdom of that decision has been borne out in recent years as it becomes apparent that the PC design – and not the mini or mainframe – will form the core of the modern office. The depth and breadth of applications available for the PCs and PC-compatible machines – along with the vast number of machines in service – has all but ensured that there will be nothing else to touch it.

The rate at which companies buy their second and third PCs is clear evidence of this. PCs are not experimental executive toys which are tried by a corporation once and forgotten about. They are purchased again and again because of the power, flexibility and standardisation that they bring to office work.

Recent statistics confirm this view. A 1985 survey by Compaq estimated that some 74 per cent of all PC buyers were repeat purchasers who had a much more sophisticated approach to their needs and a clearer idea of exactly what they want.

Perhaps not surprisingly, the largest percentage of second-time buyers were among those who purchased the new 80286 technology machines. Up to 90 per cent of Compaq 286 buyers were second-time purchasers.

PCs GO CORPORATE

The other interesting trend pointed up by recent statistics is the acceptance of the PC by the world's large corporations – who were expected to lead the world towards mainframe nirvana only a few years ago. A survey conducted by Dun and Bradstreet between 1983 and 1985 showed a direct correlation between the size of a firm and the number of PCs they used.

According to the Dun and Bradstreet survey, some 85 per cent of those working in firms that have more than 1000 employees use PCs – as opposed to only 24 per cent of those in companies with less than 19 people on staff. Although those figures represent the widest variance of PC usage in the corporate market, the average rate of PC adoption among most companies is growing steadily and stood at about 46 per cent at the time of writing.

From the outsider's point of view, the biggest question raised by all this success would have to be: 'Why did the PC succeed where so many other attempts to bring high-tech to the office failed?'

The answer seems to lie in the fact that the PC identified and then filled a desperate need in the business world – although not in the way that even IBM had expected. It turns out to be a market very much driven by its users – not by the companies which operate in it.

The planners, predictors and marketing people have NOT driven the business computer market. IBM has in the form of its PC Junior and PC Portable computers proved that even long-standing leaders in the information-processing business can fail if they don't listen to users.

What have users been saying? Overwhelmingly they have said that they want standards – in hardware, software, communications and support. The growth and development of the PC has provided them with that.

• PC hardware is now standard enough that hundreds of manufacturers and dealers can all sell machines which are compatible with one another – meaning that producers of add-on expansion boards, hard disks, modems and other hardware additions can produce equipment in large enough quantities to make them widely available and quite affordable.

There are now more than 1000 companies selling equipment compatible with the IBM PC standard – with in excess of 2500 dealers for those PCs in the US alone. US businesses invested more than $30 billion in PC companies in 1985, ensuring a healthy and competitive market.

• PC software developers can now count on a potential buying audience that totals in the millions worldwide and can thus provide the PC user with a broad choice of applications in a market competitive enough to prevent prices from getting too high. There is also now a clear growth path for software developers who want to offer new and more powerful products, but don't currently see that the hardware to support them exists at a reasonable price.

When Microsoft, for example, started work on its multi-tasking Apple Macintosh-like Microsoft Windows system the basic IBM PC usually didn't have much more than 256K of RAM memory, commonly offered only two 360K floppy disk drives and used the relatively slow 8088 processor. By the time the software was finished, however, powerful and high-speed 80286 and 8086 machines were on the market with 10, 20 and even 30 Mb internal hard disk drives. The point is that Microsoft was able to start work on Windows as an IBM PC product, but because of the growth path offered by the PC standard, could also design it so that as the power of the basic PC grew the software would take advantage of that extra power.

ADD-ON STANDARDS

The software can also count on the add-on hardware support – producing, for example, versions of Lotus 1–2–3 and Framework which take advantage of the expanded memory specifications developed by Lotus/Intel/Microsoft.

● PC communications equipment suppliers can develop networks and multi-user systems which start with IBM and DOS compatibility as a base and then move to innovate from that standard. In fact, many new dedicated multi-user systems are now designed with PC compatibility as an integral component of the system from the start. These replace the dozens of incompatible systems and proprietary architecture systems which have appeared over the years.

PCs can also act as terminals to larger mainframe and mini-computers at a very low cost per workstation. The low cost means that a PC makes for a much easier buying decision than a terminal-based system, while the high degree of connectivity and flexibility means that DP departments can 'build-up' PC-based workstations from a basic single-drive machine running a terminal emulation program into a powerful stand-alone desktop system.

● The level of technical support for PCs has also been a major factor in their success. As increasing numbers of manufacturers built machines conforming to the IBM PC design standard, it became much more likely that a given dealer – even if it didn't sell that particular brand of computer – could offer support and service for the machine. Knowing how to fix an IBM PC became as much a part of a computer technician's basic training as the inner workings of a common four-stroke engine was for the automotive mechanic.

There's no doubt that the PC phenomenon has changed the way people in business operate – quite likely changing the way you work. But if PCs are to continue their dominance in the office automation market, they will have to continue offering flexibility. And that flexibility should put the shoe on the other foot – with PCs changing the way they work instead of you having to change the way you work.

PCs AT ALL LEVELS

At the moment, there are four 'levels' of PC use into which your own needs may already fit:

1 The Personal Productivity Applications. These offer the common 'stand-alone' functions such as word-processing, database management, financial planning using spreadsheets and all the other jobs the PC is popularly conceived of handling.

2 The Inter-connective Applications. Here you are given the opportunity to share the data you have generated in the first level of application with file transfer, electronic mail, access to large mainframe databases and peripheral and file-server sharing all playing a role.

3 The Net-specific Applications. At this point the PC starts pioneering new applications which just wouldn't be possible with any other type of technology. Network-specific (as opposed to stand-alone) software will offer the ability to have file and record-locking, allow two people to look at the same data at once and exploit the full power of the 80286 (and 80386) processor technology to produce something which offers almost a minicomputer level of functionality.

4 PC Systems Integration Applications. This is the 'top-level' of PC use and will see PCs fully integrated into corporate information systems as widespread mainframe to micro links, extensive networks and corporate-wide communications systems are developed. It requires compatibility with the IBM Systems Network Architecture, 3270 terminal emulation, the IBM Token Ring Local Area Network and other IBM communications approaches.

Although these distinctions make it easier to think about the way in which the computer industry offers its applications, the design for all office-based systems should start with the needs of the business and end up with a collection of computer hardware and software that addresses those needs – not the other way around.

You will have made your original decision to buy a PC because you perceived it as a solution to a particular problem, so why throw that approach away when it comes to developing further that system? During the course of this book. we will try to help you recognise and identify your needs and choose the appropriate additions to your system which will meet them.

HOW TO USE THIS BOOK

This book is intended for everyone who uses microcomputers in business – from the slightly experienced novice who has just come to grips with a spreadsheet to the 'power user' who is thinking in terms of macros, extended memory and network link-ups.

In order to provide something which is useful to everyone in that readership, I have structured the book on three levels – each designed to accommodate the needs of an increasingly sophisticated user. If you are relatively naive about the business of selecting applications, add-ons and generally wandering through the maze of jargon which can lead so many users astray, then you should start reading the book at Part One.

PART I What else do you want to do with your PC? A look at the reasons and mechanisms for developing further applications on your micro, along with some pointers on just which applications would be most appropriate and how you go about putting those applications in a computing framework. At the start of this section (which comprises Chapters One, Two and Three), I started with the question, 'What else do you want to do with your PC?', while at the end I finish off by looking at lessons that can be learned from how others have configured their existing computer software/ hardware combinations which should help you to fulfil the requirements you have specified.

If, however, you're pretty sure of the extra jobs you need the computer to tackle, then you'll probably want to leap into the book at Part Two where I look in detail at which existing PC applications best suit the needs that you have outlined for yourself.

PART II Which application best suits your needs? By the time you reach this section (comprising Chapters Four through Twelve), you should have a pretty good notion of the types of new jobs you want the PC to handle and will be able to get an idea of which software packages are available to carry them out.

PART III Making the most of your applications. The final section of the book is really for all PC users, new, old and moderately experienced. It's a hardware reference guide which you can turn to whenever you're in a spot. While the first two portions of the book concentrate largely on PC software, the final series of appendices attempts to bring hardware considerations into perspective. The hardware flexibility of your PC brings with it a confusing array of expansion options, each of which carries its own idiosyncrasies and difficulties. This reference section should give you all the information you need to survive the selection of an extra hard disk, memory board or other major add-on without tearing your hair out.

Note
To illustrate the types of hardware technologies you will encounter, we have used specific products from leading hardware product companies in our Appendices. As sponsor of this book, and a leading P C manufacturer, Compaq's products were selected as examples in the 'How to buy a P C ' section (Appendix A), while those of Epson, AST and other leading peripheral manufacturers provide examples in subsequent Appendices.

PART I
WHAT ELSE DO YOU WANT TO DO WITH YOUR PC?

Chapter One

'Thanks, but I already have an application'

There are almost as many reasons for people limiting their use of a PC as there are for people buying one in the first place. Most people buy PCs because they perceive them as a solution to a particular and specific information-processing problem – but getting too comfortable or complacent with one application might blind you to the multitude of other tasks which can be accomplished with your machine.

This book is designed to help you make the most of your PC – to bring the full power of the machine to bear on the running of your business. And that means developing a range of specific applications to meet the wide variety of challenges which are presented in day-to-day business life.

Here I'll look at the reasons why people are reluctant to develop new applications for their business PCs and perhaps help you overcome some of your own prejudices about using a PC for more than one task.

NO TIME FOR NEW THINGS

This is the most common – and entirely understandable – reason people give for not developing new jobs for their PCs. The question, however, should not really be a question of 'making work' for your PC, but instead finding other problems that it can solve. In the short term, you may need to invest some time and effort to identify those problems. But having done so, the time you'll save by using the PC to do those jobs will more than make up for this investment.

MORE COST AND MORE HARDWARE

Some say that new applications will cost too much – in terms of both the applications themselves and the extra hardware which may be needed to run them – to consider adding to the existing expense of their systems.

This, however, is patently a false economy. If you are to undertake any new application, you would be doing so because that application would allow you to work more efficiently and more effectively. Unless you buy some esoteric application for the sake of it, there is small likelihood that any significant new business application would not offer the payoff equal to what you paid for it.

The only really major hardware add-on you would be likely to HAVE to buy is extra memory. Few applications these days will run in 128K – most need at least 256K and many need a good deal more. But prices for extra RAM these days are very cheap and they should be no real disincentive to setting up a new application.

IT WILL COMPLICATE MY LIFE

You may well believe that getting a new application will require that you learn lots of new command structures. This need not necessarily be the case. If you bring together your new suite of applications with the criteria of command continuity in mind – by doing something like buying a copy of Symphony to do small word-processing and communications jobs if you're already used to using Lotus 1–2–3. Both 1–2–3 and Symphony are very similar in command structure and Lotus files can be used in Symphony – without having to learn any great new command structure.

NO SMALL APPLICATIONS – ONLY SMALL THINKERS

The only limits on the use of your PC in the office are defined by the available software base, the responsibilities of your own job and your own enthusiasm for your work. As there are literally thousands of programs which can run on the IBM/Compaq hardware standard PC, software should not hold you back.

The major factor in the success of developing further applications is planning. In computing terms, that means taking what's known as a 'systems approach' to how you set things up – examining exactly what you want out of the system before you start.

THE PC SAID TO THE BISHOP

In my capacity as a sometimes unpaid business PC consultant to friends, friends of friends and even the odd stranger, I have come across a wide variety of people looking to develop new applications on their machines. In almost every case, the person who was planning to get a new piece of hardware or a new application already had a pretty firm idea of what they wanted – but became extremely fickle when actually committing themselves to a system which would do it.

At one time, there was a senior member of the Church of England who called me because he wanted advice on developing a database which might help keep track of his ever-moving flock of vicars and parishioners. Either through divine providence or a good deal of research, he had come up with a suggestion for a system in which the hardware was the primary consideration.

He wanted to get (and remember, this was a few years ago) a CP/M based computer from a small British manufacturer that was highly limited in how it could be expanded, but which was offered at a very low price with some cheap database software thrown in.

I suggested to him that he start by looking at the software he would need – perhaps a powerful database package such as dBase II – and then look at the hardware to run it.

He spent a good deal of time taking copious notes and asking somewhat non-ecclesiastical questions about hardware and software pricing, thanked me for the advice and went out and did what he was planning to do in the first place. That was four years ago and I understand he is now in the position of looking again for equipment and software because he's reached the limits of both the cut-price database and the underpowered PC. While I sympathise with his wish not to raid the church's coffers too much, I think there was something of a false economy in spending less in the short term only to find that you have to spend more in the long run. The moral: take the long view when weighing up the power of new software against its price. You only get what you pay for.

This common-sense way of buying and using applications is often known among people in the data-processing industry as the 'systems approach' and all it means is that you examine all your existing and likely future requirements for what a system is supposed to do – and then tailor your software and hardware buying criteria to effect the best result.

It was just such an approach which yielded excellent results for the Association of Certified Accountants of London. The group started by identifying the areas throughout its organisation – not just one department – that could benfit from use of a micro and then set about putting together the systems to fulfill those requirements. Those areas of interest are:

- Running a self-contained word-processing operation

- General invoicing and stock control

- Booking and invoicing for accountancy courses

- Creating a database to keep track of ACA membership and certificates

This idea of looking at the whole picture – instead of only one pressing problem – is the real key to the success of getting new applications for your machine. Having done so, you may find that there aren't immediate computer-based solutions to all your office information needs – or that they are not currently in a price range you can afford.

Laser printing to produce high-quality 'in-house' newsletters, for example, is something that would have cost you more than £10,000 only a few years ago – but laser printers are now inexpensive enough that you can put an entire 'desktop publishing' system into place (including a Compaq PC, software and laser printer) for between £6000 and £7000.

The ACA saw this as a possible area of development when it first looked at getting its collection of Compaqs, but at that time neither the software nor hardware was in place for this application. By early 1986, however, the company had taken delivery of two Hewlett-Packard LaserJet printers (as well as a link-up to a 'Compugraphic' typesetting machine) and used this new equipment to set up an in-house printing department.

The ACA case suggests that you shouldn't necessarily limit your thinking to what it is that you think PCs can do or to what you think you can afford. Nobody says that you have to run right out and buy the technology to solve these difficult problems right away, but by identifying them as areas of further development you can be well prepared to integrate the new applications as and when the technology either advances or becomes more affordable.

Chapter Two

Where you fit in

In this chapter we'll try and help you come to terms with your own prejudices about PC usage, frame your thoughts in order that you can develop new and more complex applications and select those new applications which will make the most use of your resources while best serving your needs.

As is often the case in these things, a multiple choice quiz can help focus your mind on the topic without forcing you to listen to a mind-numbing litany of 'shoulds' and 'shouldn'ts'. To use the quiz, read through the questions thoroughly – making sure you under-stand them properly first – then wade in. Take it seriously, because we're going to score you at the end of the quiz – giving each answer a weighted rating. Here are the questions:

1 A computer – besides being a powerful vehicle for calculation and computation – can also be an important communications medium. How does your job relate to this communications aspect of the technology. Are you responsible for?;
A) Communication within a small group or department which rarely needs to send that communication beyond the office walls
B) Co-ordination of information provided by people from a variety of groups, companies and departments – but largely for analysis and distribution within a smaller office or department
C) Development and distribution of material collected from a broad number of sources on a regular basis

2 The role you play in a business environment is defined just as much by what happens when you are there as by what goes on when you're not. What happens to your work when you're on holiday?
A) The work is left largely untouched until you get back (the work you do is pretty unique and there is little else any of your colleagues could be 'getting on with' in relation to it while you're away).
B) The areas you're responsible for are 'monitored' while you're gone – and minor updates to your computer files are made in your absence
C) The work you were looking at just before you left is completed by someone else while you're gone. New work is waiting for you when you return

3 Exactly how you apply a PC to your job really depends on just what it is you're producing or selling. Different data processing techniques and modes of operation are appropriate to selected types of enterprises. Is your work primarily concerned with?;
A) Providing a service – where it is your time, analysis and evaluation which is paramount to what you do – as opposed to any form of 'end product'
B) Manufacturing a product – where the major concern is having

tight control over stock levels, manufacturing costs and distribution methods

C) A combination of products and services which may be offered together as part of a 'range'

4 The way in which you approach PC applications – in terms of costs, the types of jobs you expect from the machine and the time that you have to put into using the machine – is partially defined by the type of company or association you are in. Would you classify yourself as?;

A) A self-employed professional (doctor, lawyer, accountant, writer, etc.) who works largely alone or with only a few other partners

B) A small business – probably selling a variety of goods and services in a small, centrally located retail or wholesale outlet

C) A member of a medium-sized corporation or company. Your role is defined by department rather than company alone

5 The type of information you handle in your day-to-day work will have a great deal of bearing on the system that's right for you – and on your choice of hardware and software. Is your work mainly involved with?;

A) Numeric and equation-related operations

B) Report-writing and text manipulation

C) A combination of the above in a specialised context (i.e. writing weekly departmental reports incorporating materials from an accounting package)

6 The size of your company will make a difference in terms of how many people may eventually need to have access to the information you process and reflect on the manner in which your information has to be prepared. How many employees are there in your firm?;

A) 1 to 10

B) 11 to 100

C) More than 100

7 No-one works completely in isolation, so whatever data management system you have must take into account the other people who

have to work with shared information. How much of the data you work with on a day-to-day basis is also worked with by your colleagues?;
A) Very little
B) A moderate amount
C) All of it

8 In medium-sized and large companies, the data processing department is the key to the operation of micros, minis and mainframes in a corporate environment. For the DP department to offer the best service possible, it must work closely with you. What sort of role does your data processing department play in your company's microcomputer operations?;
A) None – we don't have one
B) A peripheral role – PCs are treated as stand-alone devices
C) An integral role

9 In order to ensure that shared information stays in a format in which large numbers of people in a corporation can read it, there is often a company-wide policy on microcomputer software. Do you have such a policy?;
A) No, we can buy what we like
B) Yes, there is a selected list of off-the-shelf PC software we can order without getting large numbers of high-level approvals
C) Yes, but most of our software is either purchased or developed by our data-processing department

10 The purchase and use of new micro applications software requires a certain degree of commitment from those planning to undertake it. Most software that's worth buying also requires an equal investment in training and 'tailoring' to your needs. How much time do you have for this?;
A) A fair amount as I realise the investment will pay off in the long term
B) A limited amount, but I plan to phase in new applications over a period, so this shouldn't be a problem
C) Very little. Any time that I have for such things needs to be booked a good deal ahead of time and had better be worthwhile

Answering these ten questions should provide you with some

interesting insights into just how you think about applications and the kinds of commitments you will need to use them further. To 'score' this quiz, give yourself only 5 points for every 'A' answer, 10 points for every 'B' reply and 15 for a 'C' answer. When you're added up your total, you might find the following analysis helpful.

50–75 points: you use your PC very much as a Personal Computer, keep your data pretty much to yourself and should be able to develop your applications base further from existing 'off-the-shelf' PC software packages. These will probably be a library of powerful 'horizontal' applications which each accomplish one thing very well – but don't allow you to do a whole variety of jobs in each package.

75–125: you have a moderate need for transfer of data with your colleagues, are less likely to need to switch between too many jobs and will get some input from other areas of the firm about how you use your PC. You should look at either a small group of 'linked' horizontal PC applications, or consider one of the more up-market 'integrated' software packages which would allow you to use the same command sequence between each package and swap information between them.

125–150: you will be getting and developing new applications in conjunction with your data processing department. You will either have – or will be in the throes of looking at – a networking system for your office. You should look at a few, very specific and highly complex pieces of software which can deal with networks, easy inter-departmental exchange of data as well as win the approval of your DP manager.

Chapter Three

Applications the second time round

Now that you've decided to look at 'second-time' applications, you might be tempted to start thinking right away about the actual hardware and software components which are going to make up those applications. Don't give in to this temptation.

THE LAST THING YOU NEED

A few years back, a well-known UK microcomputer distributor ran an ad campaign to sell business micros and software under the slogan – 'When improving the flow of information in your office, the last thing you want to think about is a computer'. The idea was that people should be encouraged to take a considered and rational approach to office automation, rather than being lured by nice-looking hardware and snazzy-sounding software.

As a veteran PC user, I'm sure you'll agree that the ad company's approach was a little simplistic – but it did get across the message that you need to consider a lot more than getting a box with some software if you are going to make the best use of desktop computing in the office. So, rather than just piously saying that you should consider all relevant factors before buying any new PC applications – look at the following proposed plan of action. It is written for people working in a small office or department but could apply equally to someone working in a small partnership, or working in conjunction with their data-processing department in a large firm.

1 Talk to the other people in your department. Although your machine is called a Personal Computer, the information you are manipulating on your PC is likely to be developed for a good many people other than yourself. There's no point in your getting together a whole bunch of highly-impressive new applications on your PC if the information generated by those applications is not going to be available to the people you work with who need to see it. A perfect example of this type of program is a simple time-management or 'diary' program which helps you keep track of where you're going and when it is that you're going there.

Suppose, however, that you step out for coffee and a call comes in from someone wanting to make an appointment with you. Unless your secretary or colleagues are using the same diary system, they won't know where on your PC to look for the information and will leave you looking rather disorganised in the eyes of the person trying to make the appointment with you.

Suppose instead that you run a diary program, over a network of PCs with each user on the network able to access another's diary (with levels of protection built-in so that you can 'lock' certain pages or files) and thus be able to see at all times when their colleagues might be free. Such software is available and I have seen it working well in a number of companies – but you have to make the initial consultation with your workmates first if you are ever to get such a joint data-processing venture off the ground.

2 Work with your colleagues to develop a list of all the data-processing jobs which go on in the office. Having got the agreement from the people you work with that more needs to be made of the company PCs, it's probably a good idea to do a little collective 'brain-storming' about where all the office data-processing jobs are and how they could be more effectively approached if better use is to be made of the business micros.

Don't think any job too unlikely to start with – although it may well turn out that some of them just aren't worth putting anywhere else but on paper.

3 Assign particular people to investigate the merits of various hardware/software systems. Once you have put together what you think is a reasonable list of jobs for the PC to tackle, you'll need to get specific people looking at various types of software which can handle those jobs. Get them to start with the job you want to do, then find the software to do it – rather than the other way round.

4 Find areas of common interest between the applications. With a well-researched list of the computer-manageable jobs and the suggested list of applications to do those jobs, you can now cross-compare the applications listed and find areas of overlap. In many ways, the more overlap you can find the better, as it will mean that you'll be able to more easily exchange information between applications, spend less time in training and have common formats for your office data.

The action plan I've outlined here should – in step 3 – provide you with a list of office jobs which roughly break down into five categories.

Part II in general will deal with how you move from identifying jobs that fit into those categories to selecting actual pieces of 'real-world' computer software to do them. The categories are:

Financial planning (Chapter Four)

Probably the most 'high-profile' of the micro's business jobs is working with numbers and financial plans. Contrary to popular opinion, however, this is not just limited to spreadsheet modelling and clever recalculations.

Well-exploited PC-based financial planning may also encompass applications as diverse as project planning software, micro-to-mainframe communications links and presentation graphics systems. Integrated and flexible financial planning may also make use of specific accountancy software and database management systems. Your finances are not simple, so there is no reason why the software used to deal with them should be simplistic.

Keeping track (Chapters Five and Six)

The handling of computer-based records is more than just database management. Modern corporate reference systems often require quick and easy access to not only 'card-index' type of records for personnel and payroll, but also 'key-word' searches for company libraries and sometimes the ability to catalogue images as well as text. A well-rounded look at software that helps you keep track of your business must examine not only the issues in managing databases, but also the benefits of on-line services, various methods of storage and ways of bringing the 'ordering' power of databases to applications such as word-processing.

Corporate communications (Chapters Seven and Eight)

Neatness counts. The language of corporate communication is the memo and the presentation and preparation of this is covered here. I also look at how word-processors – in both stand-alone and integrated software packages – can best be used along with networks and some presentation software to provide you with the best way of getting your message across to your colleagues.

Inter-office communications (Chapter Nine)

Moving outside the confines of your own office, there are other ways of paperlessly communicating with people in other departments and the outside world. These will involve the use of local area networks, electronic mail systems and telex systems. This chapter looks at the development of those systems and how they can more effectively open your doors for business.

Presentations (Chapter Ten)

Not all business information, however, fits inside the range of letters and numbers that come in a word-processor or electronic message system. Often you will need graphic material to fully explain your idea – bar charts, line drawings and production schedules can all crystalise things in the mind in the way that no amount of description could do. This chapter looks at using business graphics systems and many of the new graphic operating environments to bring that extra polish to your work.

Putting it all together (Chapter Eleven)

These categories go beyond being simply redesigned descriptions of the major PC applications types and go some way towards bringing together the way PCs work with the way you work in your office.

PART II
WHICH APPLICATION BEST SUITS YOUR NEEDS?

Chapter Four

Financial planning

Like any job in business, the key to success is choosing the right person (or in this case hardware and software) for the right job.

It may look easy now choosing between a word-processor and a spreadsheet to develop a business plan. But what happens when you start trying to run the accounts of a small cash-based company with the PC? Do you use Lotus 1-2-3 ? PC Cash Trader? Pegasus Accounts? Perhaps an integrated package which lets you bring in a database of payroll records with your spreadsheet?

THE SYSTEMS APPROACH

The only way to choose between these similar-sounding packages is by having a very clear idea in your head about exactly what it is you want the PC to do for you.

All it means is that you build up your computer hardware and software collection with the idea in mind of developing a 'system' to accomplish specific tasks.

VERTICAL OR HORIZONTAL

Your job is to find out just how 'vertical' your needs are. Vertical software is generally understood to be software written for people engaged in a specific job or profession – ie. milk production and planning applications would be vertical software for dairy farmers OR specially-designed columnar word-processing packages would be vertical market software for script-writers.

Unfortunately, vertical software – by its very nature – only appeals to a limited market and is thus expensive and difficult to sell. This has led to the rise of the 'horizontal' package – which attempts to be all things to all users.

OFF-THE-SHELF OR TAILORMADE

There are essentially two types of horizontal software:

● easy-to-use (but limited) general purpose programs – These allow you to do work as it is defined by software engineers and hardware limitations. These include spreadsheet programs such as older versions of Microsoft Multiplan and Visicalc.

● tough-to-master (but powerful) business development packages which can be 'tailored' for various vertical tasks. Among the most powerful of these programs is Lotus 1–2–3 – which contains its own spreadsheet 'language' and allows you to develop complex information systems – although it's not that easy to use or learn right away.

Many software packages combine elements of both the above groupings, but they usually have an overall approach which falls down in one or other of the categories.

The first category of programs assumes that the software developers know what your needs are and that all you have to do is pick a pre-written package that matches those needs, while the second assumes (often quite rightly) that no software author can imagine all your exact requirements and that the best option is to offer you powerful tools to create your own application.

So far, most of the business application software for the PC is of the first type – and that's entirely appropriate. The vast majority of PC owners are coming to a computer for the first time, and they need something which is relatively easy to use and which can 'plug-in-and-go'.

Deciding which type of financial package is right for you depends a great deal on your plans for the future. It's pretty obvious that if your work with numbers and finances is likely to be limited, then you may not need more complex 'tailorable' financial packages – and that otherwise you should be looking for something which lets you do 'macros', or write in some form of 'language' to get the program to do things AND have a good deal of room in which to do it all.

INVERSE RELATIONSHIP

What many people may not understand right away is the inverse relationship between the power of the software and its ease of use. Fig. 1. opposite spells this out in plain terms – the utility of 'friendly' software drops off very shortly after using it, while it reaches a high degree of ease-of-use. The reverse is obviously true for more complex 'tailorable' packages.

You are far more likely to need 'manual' tailoring control in your software than you might expect. And the more tools there are to give you that control, the greater the likelihood that the package can meet your needs.

THE SPREADSHEET

One of the most popular financial planning tools in the micro-computer world is the spreadsheet. First developed in the form of 'Visicalc' by Dan Bricklin in the late 1970s as a way of using his Apple II computer as an 'electronic ledger', the spreadsheet has dominated much of the way people have used micros in the past ten years.

Despite the spreadsheet's popularity, however, there are still a good many fundamental rules for spreadsheet and financial modelling design which users seem to ignore. In my assessment of the most common mistakes made by users of spreadsheets, the following 'rules to plan by' have emerged:

1 Plan your model before you actually start entering on the screen. This is a little more complex and slightly less obvious than it sounds. A good spreadsheet is a careful balance between information that is row-oriented and that which is column-based. Making the wrong choice about which 'axis' you will base your spreadsheet on can lead to great difficulties in using, revising, printing and reading your financial plan. Take, for example, a simple model which uses monthly costs and income information to calculate monthly and annual profits before tax in the Psion Abacus spreadsheet.

If you decide that the months will run along the 'X' axis (the columns) and the costs, income and profit totals will run down the 'Y' (the rows) axis, the part of the sheet that you can see will look like Fig. 1 below.

	A	B	C	D	E	F	G
1							
2							
3		Jan	Feb	March	April	May	June
4							
5	Costs	90	110	100	95	130	110
6	Income	1000	1050	900	1300	1200	1100
7							
8	Profit	910	940	800	1205	1070	990
9							
10	Year total	5915					
11							
12							
13							
14							
15							
16							
17							
18							
19							
20							
?							

CELL A1   GRID USED A1:G10   TASK tst
CONTENTS EMPTY

Fig. 1

The problem is, of course, that you can only see the figures up until June – and the annual total has to be put in a place where it doesn't really make a good deal of sense. In order to read figures for the whole year, you would have to 'scroll' across the sheet – all because the greater number of factors (in this case the months) have been oriented along the top instead of the side of the spreadsheet.

Look at what happens when we change the orientation to read with the months down the left-hand side and the cost, income and profit factors along the top, as in Fig. 2 below.

```
          A         B      C      D       E    F    G
 1
 2                Income  Costs  Profits
 3
 4      January    1000    100     900
 5      February   1100    110     990
 6      March      1050     95     955
 7      April      1200     90    1110
 8      May        1300    120    1180
 9      June       1800    132    1668
10      July       1599    140    1459
11      August     2350    200    2150
12      September  1400    234    1166
13      October    1000     89     911
14      November   3000    345    2655
15      December   5000    653    4347
16
17      Total     21799   2308   19491
18
19
20
 ?

CELL A1    GRID USED A1:D17    TASK tst
CONTENTS EMPTY
```

Fig. 2

Now you can not only see the figures for each month on the screen, but also the total incomes, costs and profits at the bottom as well. This change is also reflected when you print the spreadsheet out. If you have a spreadsheet that is very long horizontally – when it need not be – you may well have to paste several sections of it together in order to get something which can be read as a whole.

On balance, a vertical spreadsheet is often more helpful than a horizontal one – but you won't know which is best until it's too late unless you do some planning beforehand.

2 Keep your formulae brief and to the point. Unfamiliarity with all the built-in functions within a spreadsheet can cause you to design its formulae in a far more complex fashion than is necessary. Take the simple function of adding up a column of cells starting at, say, B4 and extending to B16 in Fig. 3 below.

	A	B	C	D	E	F	G
1							
2							
3							
4		1200					
5		100					
6		3.67					
7		3222					
8		21					
9		213					
10		546					
11		345					
12		9865					
13		324					
14		654					
15		546					
16		453					
17							
18							
19							
20							
?							

CELL A1   GRID USED A1:B18   TASK tst
CONTENTS EMPTY

Fig. 3

You can either add these figures up by entering a formula at B18 which would run:

B4+B5+B6+B7+B8+B9+B10+B11+B12+B13+B14+B15+B16

or you can use the SUM function. The same thing as that is in the long-winded formula above can be achieved by simply writing

SUM(B4:B16). In Fig. 4, we show how both cells B18 and C18 contain the same number – while one uses the long-winded formula and the other the SUM function.

	A	B	C	D	E	F	G
1							
2							
3							
4		1200					
5		100					
6		3.67					
7		3222					
8		21					
9		213					
10		546					
11		345					
12		9865					
13		324					
14		654					
15		546					
16		453					
17							
18		17492.67					
19							
20							
?							

CELL A1   GRID USED A1:B18   TASK tst
CONTENTS EMPTY

Fig. 4

Proper use of functions will make your spreadsheets easier to read, edit and develop. The SUM function is not, however, the only one to keep in mind. There are a good many others which are far more useful and a good deal less obvious. Let's say, for example, that you wanted to get the average of all the numbers from B4 to B16 in the previous example. Without looking at the other formulae available, the obvious thing to suggest might be to add all the numbers up – which you will have done in cell B18 – and divide them by 13 (the total number of cells which are being averaged) to yield a formula something like:

B18/13

However, in most modern spreadsheets there is already an averaging function 'hardwired' into the spreadsheet so that you don't have to do all that work – or take up two cells to get one piece of information. You would just type:

AVE(B4:B16)

with AVE being the averaging command for your spreadsheets. (It varies from application to application – Psion's Abacus uses AVE, while both Symphony and Lotus 1–2–3 use AVG). It is, however, a very useful built-in command. Inserting an average into the second example we looked at would provide figures for average monthly costs with almost no extra effort (see Fig. 5 below).

	A	B	C	D	E	F
1						
2		Income	Costs	Profits		
3						
4	January	1000.00	100.00	900.00		
5	February	1100.00	110.00	990.00		
6	March	1050.00	95.00	955.00		
7	April	1200.00	90.00	1110.00		
8	May	1300.00	120.00	1180.00		
9	June	1800.00	132.00	1668.00		
10	July	1599.00	140.00	1459.00		
11	August	2350.00	200.00	2150.00		
12	September	1400.00	234.00	1166.00		
13	October	1000.00	89.00	911.00		
14	November	3000.00	345.00	2655.00		
15	December	5000.00	653.00	4347.00		
16						
17	Total	21799.00	2308.00	19491.00		
18	Monthly average	1816.58	192.33	1624.25		
19						
20						
?						

CELL A1   GRID USED A1: D18   TASK tst
CONTENTS EMPTY

Fig. 5

Both SUM and AVE are quite basic examples of how functions can be used to shorten and make more precise the way in which you write your spreadsheet models. The best functions actually take the place of quite complex formulae and replace them entirely with one-word commands.

In Lotus Symphony, for example, the list of functions includes a 'present value' calculator which is used to calculate the present value of an annuity over a given payment period, interest rate and number of payment periods.

An ordinary annuity is assumed to be a series of payments made at equally-spaced intervals and present value is the value today of the payments to be made or received later, with the value discounted at a given interest rate or discount rate. Calculating the present value of an ordinary annuity gives you a way of comparing different investment opportunities or potential obligations while taking into account the time value of money.

At any rate, this Symphony function:

@PV(payment,interest,term)

takes the place of the much more complex equation:

$$PV = payment *\frac{(1-(1+interest)-n}{interest}$$

3 When copying, inserting and moving pieces of the spreadsheet around, be extremely careful that your cell references remain 'relative'. In most spreadsheets, there are two ways to refer to a given cell – in either relative or absolute terms. In most cases, you will want to refer to it in the absolute manner for greater flexibility.

Suppose, for example, that once again you were working with the cost/income/profit model we looked at earlier and decided that you wanted to have an extra column of information which contained details on the amount of tax you had to pay each month on the income you received. The thing you would do is to use the spreadsheet's 'insert' function actually to insert the column itself and name that column (see Fig. 6 opposite).

Now you'll need to enter a formula to calculate the taxes – in this case at perhaps 30 per cent of your net profit for each month. This will give you a series of figures that looks like those in Fig. 7 opposite.

What you want to guard against, however, are two cell-referencing problems: ensuring that your year-end totals and averages are not screwed up because they now refer to cells which no longer

	A	B	C	D	E	F
1						
2		Income	Costs	Taxes	Profits	
3						
4	January	1000.00	100.00		900.00	
5	February	1100.00	110.00		990.00	
6	March	1050.00	95.00		955.00	
7	April	1200.00	90.00		1110.00	
8	May	1300.00	120.00		1180.00	
9	June	1800.00	132.00		1668.00	
10	July	1599.00	140.00		1459.00	
11	August	2350.00	200.00		2150.00	
12	September	1400.00	234.00		1166.00	
13	October	1000.00	89.00		911.00	
14	November	3000.00	345.00		2655.00	
15	December	5000.00	653.00		4347.00	
16						
17	Total	21799.00	2308.00		19491.00	
18	Monthly average	1816.58	192.33		1624.25	
19						
20						
?						

CELL A1   GRID USED A1: E18   TASK tst
CONTENTS EMPTY

Fig. 6

	A	B	C	D	E	F
1						
2		Income	Costs	Taxes	Profits	
3						
4	January	1000.00	100.00	270	900.00	
5	February	1100.00	110.00	297	990.00	
6	March	1050.00	95.00	287	955.00	
7	April	1200.00	90.00	333	1110.00	
8	May	1300.00	120.00	354	1180.00	
9	June	1800.00	132.00	500	1668.00	
10	July	1599.00	140.00	438	1459.00	
11	August	2350.00	200.00	645	2150.00	
12	September	1400.00	234.00	350	1166.00	
13	October	1000.00	89.00	273	911.00	
14	November	3000.00	345.00	797	2655.00	
15	December	5000.00	653.00	1304	4347.00	
16						
17	Total	21799.00	2308.00		19491.00	
18	Monthly average	1816.58	192.33		1624.25	
19						
20						
?						

CELL A1   GRID USED A1: E18   TASK tst
CONTENTS EMPTY

Fig. 7

contain the information they used to AND that your profit figures take into account the tax which is being taken off them.

The first is something your software may already take care of for you, but you should watch out for it. The monthly average profit, for example, used to be AVE(D4:D15), but now that the cells have moved over one column it should now read AVE(E4:E15).

The question of subtracting tax from your old totals is something you WILL have to make a formula change on. Cell E4 should now read '(B4−C4)−D4' and that change should be echoed through E5 to E15 if the new profit figures are going to reflect the bite taken out of profits by the taxman. You can then insert formulae to give total tax figures for the year and average monthly tax (see Fig. 8).

	A	B	C	D	E	F
1						
2		Income	Costs	Taxes	Profits	
3						
4	January	1000.00	100.00	270	630.00	
5	February	1100.00	110.00	297	693.00	
6	March	1050.00	95.00	287	668.50	
7	April	1200.00	90.00	333	777.00	
8	May	1300.00	120.00	354	826.00	
9	June	1800.00	132.00	500	1167.60	
10	July	1599.00	140.00	438	1021.30	
11	August	2350.00	200.00	645	1505.00	
12	September	1400.00	234.00	350	816.20	
13	October	1000.00	89.00	273	637.70	
14	November	3000.00	345.00	797	1858.50	
15	December	5000.00	653.00	1304	3042.90	
16						
17	Total	21799.00	2308.00	5847	13643.70	
18	Monthly average	1816.58	192.33	487	1136.98	
19						
20						
?						

CELL A1   GRID USED A1: E22   TASK tst
CONTENTS EMPTY

Fig. 8

4 Declare your 'variables' outside a formula. The greater number of 'undeclared variables' you leave in any one formula, the more difficult it will be to modify later. If, for example, you had one formula which calculated the price after VAT of the amount you have to pay on your calculated monthly photocopier bill; and assuming perhaps that you were paying £20 per 1000 photocopies, that VAT is 15 per cent and that cell B1 contains the number of photocopies you made, the formula might look like this:

((B1/1000)*20)*1.15

If the VAT range changes, or you have to pay more per photocopy, you will be stuck having to go in and change that equation because neither your photocopier 'per copy' rate nor the VAT rate is a declared 'variable'.

What you should do in that case is perhaps to have a section at the top of the sheet where you can declare all such fixed rates – setting B1=the rate for photocopying and B2=VAT rate. That way you will easily be able to have the spreadsheet show what happens to every equation which uses VAT when the VAT changes and what happens to your net photocopying costs when the rate/per copy goes up or down.

Having VAT as a variable also means that you can show cost without VAT, cost of VAT and cost with VAT separately – as required by H. M. Customs and Excise.

THE REAL WORLD

Now that you have an idea of the kinds of issues to consider when buying financial software and some of the issues involved in using spreadsheet applications, it's worthwhile having a look how 'real-world' off-the-shelf packages address them. Over the next few pages, you'll get some insights into the operation of Lotus 1–2–3, Microsoft Multiplan 2.0 and some of the other popular financial software tools which may face you in a computer dealership.

LIFE IN LOTUSLAND

Lotus 1–2–3 has to be the single-most popular business application for machines conforming to the IBM PC hardware design. The company estimated at one point that at least one in three PC users owned and used a copy of 1–2–3.

There are a number of reasons for this – each of which is worth bearing in mind when considering 1–2–3 for use in your financial planning:

● Lotus 1–2–3 is not just a spreadsheet with a couple of nice extras tacked onto it. It also includes database-style sort and reporting facilities along with some impressive business graphics facilities. Using a printer with graphics capabilities (such as any of the recent offerings from Epson), you can use the GRAPH program disk that comes with 1–2–3 to send those graphs to paper.

● 1–2–3 was one of the first popular pieces of software to use 'keyboard macros' – which allow you to issue a complex series of commands with a single keystroke. Macros allow you to put the machine 'on automatic pilot', with 1–2–3 being fooled into thinking that the keyboard instructions it is receiving are actually coming from the keyboard. The simplest way of getting macros is to turn on the 'keyboard tape recorder' which just allows 1–2–3 to keep track of all the keys you press and then repeat that movement when you hit a designated set of keys (i.e. you could set up a 'recording' which automatically took 1–2–3 into graphics mode and displayed an updated pictorial representation of your financial figures every time you changed them).

● By extending the 'macro' facility in Lotus 1–2–3, you can actually create new applications within the package itself.

Macros are thus a powerful tool for customising Lotus 1–2–3 and really allow you to make it into quite a different package than it is when you first start using it. In fact, there are companies who set up whole businesses to do just that.

OptionWare's OptionWord+ for 1–2–3, for example, puts a word-processor, appointment scheduler, form letter system and 'desktop calculator' into the package just using its own programming capabilities. Such applications are developed not by using 1–2–3 as a keystroke recorder, but instead by using its 'programming' option for macros – with allows you to set up a series of macro actions and edit them as you would a program.

As you can see from the macros, Lotus 1–2–3 is a complex product – even experienced users often have a considerable number of questions about how best to use it. According to Lotus (on its Telecom Gold 'World of Lotus' service), some of those most commonly-asked questions include:

Q: Are Symphony files compatible with those of 1–2–3?
A: You can read a file in Symphony that was created in 1–2–3, but not vice versa. Symphony has different formulae, its macro language uses different commands, and the file format is also slightly different.

Q: When I type DIR in DOS to check the sizes of my files, then recheck the size in 1–2–3, the file size of the spreadsheet is larger than the file size DOS tells me.
A: Due to additional overhead, the size of a file can increase when retrieved. Examples of overhead not seen in the directory are range names, print settings cell pointers.

Q: I keep my Lotus files in a sub directory called Lotus and my worksheet in a directory called Lotus files. When I am in the file manager, I am unable to find my spreadsheets.
A: This is because the File Manager Utility is unable to use subdirectories. The only files it can read are those which are in the Lotus directory.

Q: Do I have to put DOS on my disks?
A: It is not necessary to put DOS on your 1–2–3 disks as long as you aren't using the FILE MANAGER or DISK MANAGER programs, both of which use DOS commands. An example is the DISK MANAGER'S 'Prepare' option which uses the DOS FORMAT command. To use the FILE or DISK MANAGER, DOS must be copied via the installation procedure.

Q: Sometimes when I use functions that compare or evaluate two numbers, the comparison comes up false, even though the numbers on the screen are equal. Why?
A: This happens because 1–2–3 stores all numbers internally to 15 decimal places. Thus 2.00 on the screen could actually be 2.0000001 internally. If the @IF function were used to compare these two numbers, the result would be false. The solution is to use the @ROUND function to round off numbers to exact amounts – especially important if the numbers are a result of calculations using division, sine, cosine, square root, etc. which often change the very first decimal place by one digit or so.

Q: When I try to input information into my worksheet I get a MEMORY FULL error. What's the problem? I bought plenty of memory.

A: This problem may happen if you have gone too far in one direction on your worksheet either horizontally or vertically. Press [END] [HOME] to bring the cursor to the last cell that utilizes memory. If you find yourself way off in 'no man's land' you have probably formatted a cell in a position that is not being used or put information into a cell and then erased it, both of which use memory.

If this is the source of your Memory Full error, do a File Xtract of the pertinent worksheet area, give it a new name, and use that new file.

The last question is particularly interesting in view of recent developments by some of the competitors to Lotus Development. The reason that your PC may be fooled into thinking it has used up all the available memory (when – in fact – only an errant variable has scattered a zero to cell IV2000) has to do with the way it handles memory.

Lotus operates by setting aside as much memory as it would need to fill all the cells between the top left-hand cell (usually A1) and the last cell that it can find in the bottom right-hand corner. So if your sheet has a cell filled with a zero, one or some other inconsequential value way off 'in the back of beyond' that could well cause you to run out of memory very quickly. Although this problem has not yet been fully addressed by Lotus itself, longtime Lotus competitor Microsoft looks to have it licked in Multiplan 3.0.

MICROSOFT AND MULTIPLAN SEQUELS

One of the notable side-effects of 1–2–3's success has been to influence the way its competitors offer their products. Microsoft's Multiplan, for example, has been influenced in a big way by the advent of Lotus 1–2–3. For the first few months of its life on the market, the Lotus product faced tough competition from Multiplan and in short order won through to the top of the charts.

This prompted a re-think by Microsoft, which in 1986 relaunched Multiplan with Version 2.0. The new offering could read files written on Lotus 1–2–3, could (like the new version of 1–2–3 itself) use the Lotus/Intel expanded memory specification (for more on this see the Appendix section), had Lotus-style macros and allowed for operation with a 'mouse'. The other new feature – and this is something you will find increasingly important as software becomes more and more dependent on computer memory – Multiplan Version 2.0 uses a 'sparse matrix' technique to conserve memory.

In some spreadsheets, for example, if you have a sheet measuring 26 columns by 26 rows into which you placed a single digit at cell Z26, the package would register that the sheet was full.

Like Lotus 1–2–3, many spreadsheets find the farthest-afield place that you've put your data and reserve all the space above and to the left of it. That can cause real problems if you happen to stick a number in a far-flung cell by mistake – telling you that you're out of !memory when hardly any information is in the sheet.

Sparse memory programs overcome this by retaining only information about where a piece of data is and what its value is – it doesn't keep hold of information about all the empty cells in-between. This frees up lots more memory and means that your financial models run much faster and more freely.

The Multiplan worksheet consists of a grid of up to 255 columns in width, and 4095 rows in length. The screen has one or more 'windows' into the worksheet, and an area showing command, message, and status lines.

The message line suggests the action to be taken, or explains errors when they occur. The status line displays coordinates of the active cell, its contents, percentage of storage remaining, and worksheet name. There is a highlighted 'active cell' on the work-sheet.

The highlight can be moved around by pressing the direction keys. The same keys are also used for scrolling the contents of windows. The Home key may be used to go to row 1 column 1 quickly. Unlike Lotus 1–2–3 and most other recently-released spreadsheets, Multiplan uses the more descriptive R1C1-style (row one, column one) cell notation.

Multiplan's command menu offers a choice of commands. To give you a flavour of the command structure and feel of Multiplan, here's how you would get going to use it on a spreadsheet model:

1 Select an active cell. The direction keys may be used. The same keys also scroll the worksheet in the window.

2 Select a command. There are two ways to do this. You can move the highlight to a command word using the space or backspace keys and then press RETURN. Or, type the first letter of the command word. A new and more specific command menu or the parameter fields with the proposed responses will be displayed.

3 Specify the parameters of the command. The TAB key may be used to move from field to field.

4 You may use the Cancel key at any time to return to the main menu.

5 Press RETURN. The command is now carried out.

With macros, descriptive cell-referencing and sparse memory-management Multiplan 3.0 has got to be worthwhile looking at as an alternative to Lotus 1–2–3. As it also has full file compatibility with the Lotus product and Microsoft has removed copy protection, it may well be a tough competitor to 1–2–3 by the time you read this. Whenever you buy, however, Multiplan will be worth considering.

PROJECT PLANNING

Spreadsheets, however, are not the only type of financial planning software at your fingertips. A healthy variety of project planning software is also available and is designed to allow your average entrepreneur to turn projects – financial and otherwise – into a reality.

Such software doesn't act as the formulator of a project (so it won't make you your first million) – it simply monitors the progress of a project that has already been planned with rigid structures and dates. This allows you to keep both a close eye on costs and progress.

Using a variety of analysis techniques, this application will cope with the schedule of most projects, however complex, breaking them down into component parts. It will then show at a glance the most important elements and an appropriate time scale for the project (a process called the critical path analysis).

The attraction of this type of program is its ability to dissect and re-assemble the project to find the quickest and/or most cost efficient route to completing the project.

There are six steps to critical path analysis:

1 Project structure: you must divide the project into easily handled component parts so the PC can show the relationships between the parts and give a diagram of them.

2 Overall duration: the PC will apply the first stage to determine the length of time that each part will take.

3 Critical path: the second stage is used to identify the key elements of the project which determine the overall duration.

4 Spare time: the project is reviewed to find which components have the freedom to be extended or delayed.

5 Balance: links between the project components are rearranged to take maximum advantage of any spare time available.

6 Presentation: the PC produces a bar chart with which you can communicate the final sequence and schedule of the project to others.

Through the graphic chain of events that is produced you can easily see which are the most important activities, and therefore deserve the most attention, and which activities have time to spare.

Chapter Five

Keeping track

Developing applications to keep track of large amounts of information is more than just a simple matter of choosing a database. In fact, many data management programs are not called databases, but 'filers' or 'data handlers'.

There are essentially four types of application which can help you file your on-line information:

1 Simple 'filer' programs.

2 Low-cost databases with severe limitations on how much they can fit.

3 Mainstream database products – led by Ashton-Tate's dBase II and dBase III – which offer programmability and powerful sorting functions.

4 Full 'relational' database software which allows sorting across a couple of databases.

Once you have selected a database from one of these four main types, you need to start thinking about how to use it. Here are a few hints:

COMPLEX BUSINESS

Databases are possibly the most difficult of mainstream PC applications to learn, but arguably the most powerful. It's probably a good idea to define terms before getting into the relatively complex business of database design. If you plan to work with a database on a regular basis, you're going to have enough to think about without having to worry about remembering what a 'field', or a 'record' actually means.

If you're already clear on what these terms mean, bear with me for a few paragraphs as I would rather spell things out – instead of under-explaining them out of some vague sense of not wanting to patronise you.

FIELDS Fields are simply the types of information you enter or retrieve from your database. The most often used example from a non-computer database, the address book, is that the headings for NAME, ADDRESS and PHONE NUMBER can all be described as headings for the fields. In an address book, the entries are usually organised in alphabetical order according to the last name of the people in the 'NAME' field.

If you wanted to find a person's phone number by looking up their address, or had a phone number jotted down somewhere but couldn't remember who it matched, you would have a very hard time. In a computer database the field names give you the opportunity of finding information through any one of a number of fact types or 'fields'. So if you had a database containing your address book, you could just as quickly type an inquiry to the database using a phone number which yielded a name as you could using a name to find a phone number.

RECORDS Records are the facts contained within all of the fields. Again, in an address book, the records would be the actual names, addresses and phone numbers which you entered into it. It will soon become clear, however, that for your records to be at all useful you will have to be very clear about which fields to use in creating and maintaining your database.

Elements within your records should be as short and precise as possible. Your database will be a mess if you try and stuff lots of unrelated information in a single record element, when you could just as easily create another field for that information. Imprecise use of computer record elements is like creating a 'miscellaneous' file in an ordinary filing cabinet and expecting to be able to find precisely where things are in that file.

AN EXAMPLE:
Name: Howard Jones
Address: 123 Anywhere St, New York
Phone: 350-4567

In the above example – which would be considered one record – the words Name, Address and Phone represent field names, while 'Howard Jones', '123 Anywhere St, New York', and '350–4567' are elements of the record. This record contains three elements, each filling in a blank opposite the field name.

With any confusion about records, fields and record elements hopefully cleared up, it's worth talking about a few basic principles of database design. Each of the four rules is pretty much common sense, but all can easily be forgotten in the rush to get a database together quickly. Time spent designing the database now pays off hansomely when you've got to use it later.

RULES TO DATABASE BY

RULE 1 Be very clear about what you want the database to do. It's often hard to tell whether you really want to be using a database or a spreadsheet to develop a model for storing some information – so think carefully about the type of information you want to store. If it's mainly names, dates, telephone numbers, place names or general comments which aren't going to deal much with changing numeric values, then a database is probably best – but if there's lots of recalculation or forecasting involved, then leave the information to the spreadsheet.

RULE 2 List every conceivable type of information you may want to include. This will help establish your field names. Try filling a few blank records on paper and see what kinds of record elements you're ending up with. If, for example, you've got a field name designating address – think whether you want street names, postal codes and city and country; if you design the database so that '123 Anywhere St, New York, UPG 1WA, USA' is all one record, then you'll never be able to sort the address out by country, postal code or city.

It doesn't matter if your list of field names looks long and absurd to begin with – it needs to be as specific as possible to begin with. You can trim it and prune it later if needed, but adding fields is more difficult than subtracting them.

RULE 3 Keep in mind the types of information you have in each field. It's no good having numbers entered as part of a 'text' field and expecting that database to be able to sort those numbers according to value.

RULE 4 Give yourself a rough estimate of the size of each record. When you start 'making' the database, you'll have to tell the database how much space you want to set aside for each field name. Although it's a good idea to keep such records sizes as tight as possible, don't let that size get in the way of giving you enough room properly to enter the record. Many people tend to short-change themselves on field name sizes – particularly when it comes to proper names and place names, which can vary in length a great deal.

DATABASE DEDICATION

There are, of course, a growing choice of databases which are available for PCs. One of the most popular is still Ashton-Tate's dBase – now in its incarnation as dBase III and dBase III plus. The

16-bit dBase III version was launched in 1984 and was enhanced in 1986 as dBase III Plus, with facilities for linking into networks.

As with most of the earlier versions of dBase, the dBase III family has maintained special popularity among people who want to use it to develop their own specific applications with its built-in programming language. Using the 'Plus' version of the software, you can also 'lock' individual records so you don't have two users trying to change the same record at the same time.

At the base of dBase III and III Plus, however, is still essentially the same dBase II program Ashton-Tate started life with in the late 1970s. As it's the most popular of the databases, you would do well to have a good grounding in it.

The first thing you should know about the dBase family is that it's as much a language in which to create your own database applications as it is an application itself. To use dBase, you first have to learn the rudiments of the command system involved with it (on dBase III and dBase III Plus, there is a 'help' structure included which insulates you to some extent from the command structure – but you would still benefit from knowing how it works if you're to get the most out of the dBase software).

The most important keywords in the dBase programming 'language' are:

CREATE In order to use a database in dBase, you first have to create one. The CREATE command asks you what you want to call the database, then opens a disk file into which all your dBase operations will run. The system then inquires how you want the records in your database to be structured and what field names you wish to have in each record. The latter question needs to be filled out with the field name first, followed by the type (character, numeric and logical), width (in number of characters) and the number of decimal places which you want numeric fields to give. When you've finished entering all the fields, just press the RETURN or ENTER key for the last field and the database will be created.

USE Once you have created the database on disk, you have to enter another command actually to use it. The command takes the form USE followed by the name of the database you want to use. Having given the USE command, you can now actually start entering information into the database.

APPEND This is the major command used for append, or adding actual data to your dBase database. It is the most common way of actually creating the records which make up the dBase II database.

LIST Once you have added a bunch of records to a dBase database (and saved them using the CTRL W option), you can type all the records you have typed in to the screen by giving the LIST ALL command. This simply lists all the entries on the database currently in use. LIST is more powerful, however, when used to do some primary sorting on the database. In a database, for example, which included among its field names LAST NAME and POST DISTRICT the command:

LIST all for LAST NAME='Smith'.AND.POST DISTRICT='NW6'

would list to the screen all the records which contained people whose last name was Smith and who lived in the postal district of NW6.

SORT SORT is the command used to put the whole database in the order you want to work with it in. USEing an existing database, you SORT ON that database with a give field to create a new database. To sort on a database called 'DEMO' in the hope of producing an alphabetical list of conference attendees by last name, you might type:

SORT on LAST NAME to NAMES

which would produce a new sorted database called NAMES.
    To look at the new sorted database, you would type:

USE NAMES

and then LIST this new database to see the new sorted file. This, of course, does not give you a nicely-formatted look at the 'forms' which make up each record. You would need to use the BROWSE command to get at that.

BROWSE This command – as you might suspect – allows you edit, add to and remove information from all the records in the database you currently have open.

INDEX Although you can use SORT, or LIST to either order files or get out certain fields within a record, you might find this rather boring if you had to do it repeatedly. To make ordering the database a lot easier, dBase provides the INDEX command. When you give this command, you create an unique INDEX file to be associated with that database.

On the DEMO file we spoke of earlier, you might give the INDEX command as:

INDEX on LAST NAME to DEMO.NDX

which would then go away and index all the records in the file on the basis on the last name, so that whenever you wanted to use and list the DEMO database according to last name you would have only to type:

USE DEMO INDEX DEMO
LIST LAST NAME, FIRST NAME, ADDRESS

You can also use the INDEX command to specify a 'secondary' index so that your database would first sort all the records by last name, then when two last names were the same the database would sort them alphabetically.

Although most of these commands seem to be simple common-sense orders, they are not supported by a good deal of on-screen help.

Most versions of dBase do have a HELP command (including the earlier 16-bit versions of dBase II), while dBase III and all further versions of the software include something called 'ASSIST' which uses menus and on-screen choices to allow you to issue many of the commands without constantly referring to the dBase manual.

The real power of the system comes into play, however, when you want to develop the relationships between the different databases. You can, for example, use two databases (which have a common field such as addresses) at once – designating one as the primary database and the other as secondary. Using the sequence of commands below, for example, you could run two databases at once, one called DEMO (the primary) and the other known as ADDRESSES (the secondary):

USE DEMO
SELECT SECONDARY
USE ADDRESSES
SELECT PRIMARY

which opens the DEMO database file, selects a secondary area, then USES the ADDRESSES file to fill that and the moves back to DEMO database via the SELECT PRIMARY command.

This method does, however, have its limitations as you do need to remember how to juggle two databases at once in order to make the most of it – and with the 'unfriendly' command structure in dBase, that's not often easy. There are, however, many new database packages on the market which do address the problem of both using multiple databases and providing an easier-to-use 'interface'.

Chapter Six

Beyond filing

Developing a database is never an easy task. And at some point a large database will evolve beyond the 'big filing cabinet' model which so many software houses suggest their software approximates.

After all, a filing cabinet doesn't let you 'sort' on more than one criteria at once, nor does it allow you to look in two filing cabinets at once. More powerful modern databases, however, do provide these facilities and deserve to be looked at in a context of their own. In this chapter I'll try and sketch out that context and give you a feel for some of the products which fit into it.

While the dBase product is aging somewhat, dBase III Plus is definitely a candidate for one of the most powerful databases you can buy. Its specifications offer the capacity for up to 1 billion records, a maximum record size of 512K and a limit on fields of 128.

Up to 15 files can be open at any one time with a limit to ten database files that can be USEd at once. On top of that, however, you should recognise that seven open 'index files' are allowed per active database file and that you can have one open format file per active database file – providing a massive degree of flexibility in just how many databases you can use at once and the kinds of operations you can carry out on them when they are open.

And although the 'Plus' version of dBase III does provide the 'Assist' command system for you in pull-down menu form, the command language in this iteration of the now-famous software is one of its most powerful. Not only are there now more commands in 'single-user' mode, but dBase III Plus also provides extensive multi-user and networking facilities so that records and files can be put through a rigorous security system to ensure that only the right people on the network get access to the right dBase files.

The flexibility which made the old dBase II and III programs so popular has not, however, been lost in all the powering-up and sprucing-up. In fact, the programming language is so powerful and flexible that you can design 'turnkey' systems around dBase III to allow your dBase III Plus-written 'vertical' to be used on its own as a 'stand-alone' package.

Auto-start facilities are available so that your own programs written in the dBase III Plus programming language can be loaded when someone first starts the machine at the beginning of the day – without them ever having to know anything about how to use dBase III except in how it relates to the program you have written.

DBase III, however, is no longer the only major player in the 16-bit database market. In recent years, Ansa Software's Paradox database – which offers the ability to 'read' dBase III files – has gained a large degree of popularity among PC database users.

STATE OF THE ART

Paradox claims to combine dBase-type power with Lotus 1–2–3 style ease of use. In terms of on-screen style, it looks a good deal like 1–2–3 and thus should be relatively easy to use for people already familiar with the Lotus product.

Unlike Lotus, however, Paradox doesn't make you keep all your data in memory and you can have as much information as you can fit on disk. Using a 'virtual memory' system, Paradox keeps as much as it can in RAM and when it runs out of room sends the rest to disk.

The major features of the package are:

• It can contain any information you might otherwise put in a list, table or form. The entries can be word, numbers, currency or dates.

• Inclusion of pre-written 'examples' which allow you to carry out the use of mailing lists, personnel records, inventories, payables and receivables, accounts and customer, client and supplier lists.

• It offers potential storage of Megabytes of information per Paradox 'table', 65000 rows, 255 columns, a maximum of 4000 characters per record and 255 characters per field.

• Query statements remain 'active' until you take action to erase them. This means that when you extract information from a table, that information isn't lost as soon as you make another query.

• A visual presentation system is used. You can move things around on the screen so that your queries, reports and forms will give you a What You See Is What You Get (WYSIWYG) result.

• A built-in programming language *à la* dBase is used. The Paradox PAL (Paradox Application Language) is used to allow 'power users' to do what they want with the package – and tailor it to their needs.

Given the growing popularity of this form of database – and the fact that it can use database files from the dBase family, it – and products like it – will have to be among the database options you consider when updating your data management products over the coming months and years.

THE PROTECTION BUSINESS

Whichever database you use, you will have to keep that software on the right side of the law. In the UK that means keeping on the right side of the 1985 Data Protection Act, which went into force on May 11, 1986.

According to the Data Protection Registrar – established in 1985 to administer the Data Protection Act – almost all UK database users should think about registering under the terms of the Act. It applies to any computer users who hold information about people or companies (and there can't be many who don't fall into this category). To get an idea of just how comprehensive its requirements are, look at the following excerpt from a Data Protection Registrar guide to the Act:

QUESTION: It is possible for a person to use personal data without himself being a Data User within the scope of the Act?

ANSWER: yes, this is possible. If the person is merely allowed to use the data, but does not himself control the contents, use and collection of the data, then he is not a Data User...A Data User who allows other persons to use his personal data in this way should ensure that the purpose of that use is described in his application for registration.

The structure of the Act is quite specific and allows few 'loopholes' against registering. It is primarily designed to ensure that people can get access to information about them that is held on computer systems – and either challenge or correct that information if they consider it incorrect or insulting.

This 'freedom-of-information' philosophy is obviously the thrust of the Act, but you would do well to realise that it only covers information held on your computer. If, for example, you had a small database of relatively sensitive material (i.e. personal impressions of job applicants) that you didn't wish to disclose, you would be well advised actually to print-out the sensitive material and then erase it from your disk. As long as information isn't held on the computer, it isn't covered by the terms of the Act.

I would advise anyone using a database in the UK to check the legislation in this area. In the UK, write to:

The Office of the Data Protection Registrar
Springfield House
Water Lane, Wilmslow
Cheshire SK9 5AX

Chapter Seven

Corporate communications

Despite the fact that PCs offer a state-of-the-art method of communicating without paper, most people within your company are still likely to want to receive information on paper. To do that effectively, word-processing software (along with a decent printer) is your best choice.

You don't need me to tell you what a word-processor is and what it's supposed to do, so I'd like to start this chapter by giving you some pointers about what to look for in a good W/P.

WORD-PROCESSOR PROFILES

The venerable Micropro Wordstar, Word Perfect and the zappy new Microsoft Word II (with mouse input device, 'windowing' and 'icon' cursor movement) have a high profile in the market – while old standbys such as Softword Systems' Multimate and Perfect's Perfect Writer get comparatively little media attention.

Despite this, all of the above packages have been recognised as powerful and well-written word-processors for the IBM PC and sold in large numbers. Although word-processors were available for the IBM PC from its introduction, it wasn't until about two years ago that we started to see the appearance of packages which could really take advantage of the machine's 16-bit design and the operating system which went with that design. Until that time, most of the word-processing products for the PC had been programs written for older 8-bit CP/M operating system computers which had been converted for the PC.

This conversion – often from Apple II versions – meant that 16-bit editions of some 8-bit programs actually ran slower and were less powerful than in their original form. The reason for this was partially because some software houses hadn't firmly come to grips with MS-DOS and partially because a conversion was safe, easy and a cheap thing to do.

To get an idea of what this new breed of 16-bit word-processing software can include, look at this list of Multimate features;

- A library of more than 50 keyboard commands.
- A menu-driven system of executing major tasks
- Document summaries which make housekeeping much easier (including author's name, date, etc.)
- A 'page-driven' disk management system which automatically saves your document every time you begin a new page (and which is economic on memory as it means you only have to have the text for one page in RAM at any one time).
- A 'mail-merge' facility which makes form-letters easy.
- An 80,000-word Anglicised word 'dictionary' for the program's spell-checker
- A huge list of printer drivers handling all the popular daisywheel and dot-matrix printers

- An 'online' system of Help menus
- And a 'key procedure' function which allows you to build-up your own keyboard 'macros' for commonly used headings, phrases and document layouts.

These are only some of the program's features and go a long way towards demonstrating the complexity and flexibility of modern W/P packages. Often, however, it's not that which impresses users – it's the fact that they can quickly learn to use the program for their own specific job.

Even a popular package like Multimate, however, has its detractors which suggest that the packages's command key combinations are not perhaps as obvious as they should have been (ie. since when is ALT–3 an obvious choice for printing?).

Each function key can have up to four different meanings – depending on which keys you press it with. While this means that all the commands are centralised, it also means that it's relatively easy to confuse Save (pressing Shift and Function key 10) with Spell Edit (pressing Function key 10 in combination with the ALT key). Keep this in mind when looking for a word-processor, as easy-to-remember command sequences can be important.

A confusing array of commands is at the heart of any powerful and successful microcomputer applications package on the market today.

The only way users can properly decide whether Multimate will aid in their work is if they look at the way it's structured and can make a judgement as to whether that fits in with the way they work.

Besides the power and complexity of modern word-processing software, another feature which closely defines the structure of the program is the 'spell-checker'. It's now common for packages such as Wordstar, Word and Multimate to offer 'dictionaries' of more than 50,000 words.

The spell-checker works by comparing all the words in a given document to those in its dictionary – and then highlighting those which don't appear in the dictionary. As it checks the spelling, it also provides the user with a word count (a handy feature for writers). The spell-checker also allows you to add proper nouns and other idiosyncratic words to create your own personal dictionary

How much a user makes of this facility again depends on the company's orientation. It's frankly not worth running short documents through a spell-checker, as it takes more time than it would to check them manually – but on a long report or book chapter the spell-checker is well worth employing.

Again speed becomes a factor, as all documents are 'spooled' from disk and the spell-checker's own dictionary must be read from disk. If you don't have a hard disk and a fast processor, you could end up with the odd inadvertent tea break while you wait for a long document to be checked.

There is an argument, however, which suggests that the whole idea of spell-checkers is anathema to good office work.

Another feature to look for is delayed printing, or print-spooling. The latter is preferred, although some programs which don't offer 'spooling' (working on one document while another is printing), do provide a print 'queue' into which a number of documents can be placed for a single print run.

The idea is that you delay printing documents out until you've got a certain number – at which point you get them all to print out one after the other while you have your tea break. This doesn't necessarily save any time, but it does allow you to organise more easily your working hours.

The most noticeable and immediate feature to look for in a word-processor is WYSIWYG (What You See Is What You Get) – or you'll have to use your imagination to envision some of the printing features (such as double, or triple spacing).

This is not necessarily a bad thing. You'll find, for example, that if a word-processor does show double or triple spacing on-screen that there would only be a few lines of text shown on screen at any one time – making the document that much more difficult to work on. Programs that don't offer WYSIWYG on line spacing are designed to show the maximum amount of your work on the screen and also forego much of the 'help' information that is normally displayed at the top and bottom of the screen.

Before you select and master a word-processor, however, you might consider how well it will fit in with the other types of data preparation systems in your office. It can take some two days to learn the basics of using a spreadsheet package properly, and much longer to learn how to exploit all of its advanced features.

WORD-PROCESSORS AND OTHER SOFTWARE

Worse, you then have to learn a completely different set of commands for each new applications package. Many packages that attempt almost the same thing will work in completely different ways, and should you try to buy the most suitable database, word-processing and spreadsheet packages they will probably have commands and features that are totally different from each other.

It also means that such software is poor for internal corporate communications, as exchanging data between one package and another is difficult. Software thus imposes artificial restrictions on the way people work with computers. People generally do not work at one job all the way through, but instead tend to skip from one task to another.

It is for that reason that new and more powerful word-processors are being designed with those sorts of added-in features coming as 'standard equipment'.

New versions of packages such as Wordstar 2000 and Perfect Writer now include communications functions so that word-processed documents can be sent via 'electronic mail' to an internal company mailbox, or to an outside communications service such as Telecom Gold – all without leaving the word-processing package.

To get an idea of what you can expect to find in a 'state-of-the-art' word-processor, we have provided the review of Microsoft's Word III word-processing package below, which should go some way to letting you know what to expect in a 'modern' W/P.

Word III

In its bid to gain a bigger slice of the word-processing market from the awesome Wordstar and the increasingly popular Multimate, Microsoft has recently released a third, yet more advanced version of its increasingly popular Word program.

Designed for the serious user who requires more advanced facilities than basic word processors and integrated packages can offer, Version 3.0 of Microsoft Word is unlike any other program available for the IBM PC.

Using Word for the first time you may find it slightly more

complex than others you may have tried. There are some word-processors which you can load up and use quite happily without reference to the manual – Word is definitely not one of them.

Few of the commands are logically abbreviated, so it takes quite a while to get used to which commands do what. (T)RANSFER, for example, is the command used to access basic functions such as loading and saving – not the first word which comes to mind.

Installing the program is comparatively easy – although the instructions in the manual are a little long-winded. Better to have too much information, however, than not enough. Version III of Word also includes Microsoft's award-winning on-disk tutorial system – which takes you through each of the features of the program. Again, it is a little too extensive for many experienced users – but would probably prove a godsend for the untutored word-processing operator.

The manuals appear to have been written like a novel, to be read from start to finish before you get a full picture of the story. In fact the introductory chapter suggests you do just this.

Thankfully the program itself, once you master the basics, is excellent. The working area is enclosed in a neat rectangular frame to the top of the screen, with a selection of commands below. It can be used with, or without a mouse – those who have a rodent swear by it, those who don't swear at it. But whichever you choose, you will undoubtedly find the commands available are a puzzle at first.

This is a simple reason for this – 17 commands are displayed below the text area, and in order to make selection as easy as possible, each starts with a different letter. To save a file on screen, you have to select TRANSFER (using the mouse or the Escape key and space bar).

A classic example of this is the new word count option. In order to count the words in a document, you must first save the file, then select LIBRARY from the list of options.

This will reveal another list of commands from which you select RUN, before typing in WC and the name of the file you're working on. The machine then loads another program, clearing the screen and giving the number of words. Finally it reloads windows and represents your work on the screen. Perhaps the copyright notice that accompanies the word count explains its primitive nature – it's dated 1981,2.

Word on the IBM is still regarded as inferior to its Apple Macintosh partner, since it uses icons, pull-down menus, and has the ability to show every font on screen. But, presentation aside, the latest version of Word on the IBM has many more superior facilities.

Compared with Microsoft's own Microsoft Write under the Windows operating environment, Word is a lot more powerful in terms of text manipulation, but in practical terms the lists of options at the bottom of the screen are not so easy to select as pull-down menus, particularly if you don't have a mouse.

Where Word III really stands out, however, is in its selection of printer drivers. A massive number are included – with a good variety of high-quality dot-matrix printers and laser printers being among them. Word III is definitely designed for both the office of the present and the future – with all the currently-popular printers, as well as the latest, included among the 'output device' lists.

Like previous versions of Word, Word III has a 'split-window' facility that allows you to jump between a number of different windows – viewing different sections of a document at once. It is useful for making notes while you work, or transferring text from an old document in one window to your letter or report in another.

The screen can be split horizontally or vertically, with up to eight frames on it at once. As you can imagine this would leave very little room in each frame to see what you're doing – but the flexibility provided by this feature means that you can very much tailor Word III to your needs.

Word III is also very much a WYSIWYG word-processor, with the appropriate graphics interfaces allowing you to show special typeface effects on-screen.

Keyboard commands – other than those on the bottom line of the screen – are relatively logical. The DELETE key, for example, is actually used for its intended purpose.in Word III – to delete the word at the cursor.

As we have said before, you are also offered the option of completely breaking away from keyboard commands and can issue almost all the commands in Word III via a mouse. As Microsoft has been heavily involved in Macintosh software development and was one of the first companies to produce its own mouse for the PC, users have come to expect a high degree of competence in mouse integration on Microsoft applications products – and

Word III will not disappoint.

Word III not only offers flexible use of either keyboard or mouse control, but follows the trend of many other recent word-processing options and adds a good many other functions on top of the basic job of processing words.

In addition to the huge spelling-checker/dictionary that Microsoft had already added to Word II (and which has been even further improved in Word III), Microsoft has improved the foot-noting commands and added a Framework-style 'outlining' facility that makes it perfect for designing point-form documents and speeches.

Word III requires a minimum of 256K RAM memory and two disk drives (preferably one of which is a hard disk). Like most other new offerings, it performs best on a more powerful hardware configuration and might be thought to be a little 'slow' while running on a standard twin-drive 4.77 Mhz PC (sort of like driving a Ferrari in town traffic).

In recognition of the increasing importance of inter-office communication, Word III will also be available for networked systems as well as single-user machines. And there are no elaborate copy-protection schemes to mess up your use of the software – Microsoft has removed copy protection on all new applications software releases.

In the end one simply has to accept that Word is probably the most advanced word processor to date in terms of features, flexibility and power – which also means it's one of the most complex to use.

And because many of those facilities are 'foward-looking' things such as mouse control, operation with laser printers, support for networks and the kinds of large-dictionary spell-checkers which the newer and more powerful 80286 and 80386 machines can take advantage of, we have to conclude that Word III's extra power will not go to waste and that it will grow with your hardware. The more memory, speed and communication you add to your PC system, the more Word III will take advantage of that.

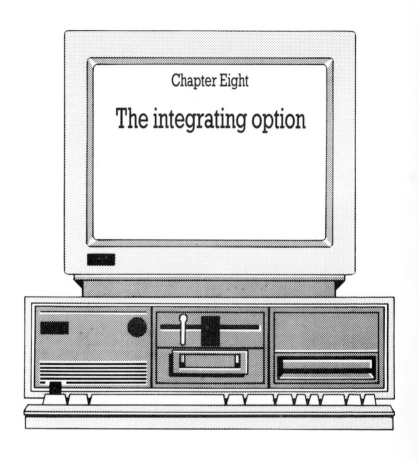

Chapter Eight

The integrating option

It is a waste of time to have to enter what amounts to the same information two or three times onto the same computer simply because it has to be manipulated in two or three different ways.

Consideration of this problem has led the software industry to invest considerable time and effort over the last three years in finding ways to 'integrate' general applications software so you can easily skip from one job to another and transfer data between applications. Such software usually includes at least a word-processor, database and spreadsheet – and often also offers on-screen business graphics and communications facilities.

The sheer scope of integrated software offers a bewildering choice to the potential user. It is, however, an important choice, since buying integrated software implies a commitment to a particular standard. That standard gets you round the data incompatibility problems inherent in using unconnected stand-alone packages.

Anyone who uses a collection of packages soon discovers the frustration of being in the middle of a program while doing, say, a spreadsheet, and requiring information from a file held on one of the others (such as the database). In these circumstances, you have to exit the program, load the new program, find the data, write it down on a piece of paper, re-load the spreadsheet and start modelling again.

Integration means getting applications to relate to each other so that you have the ability to transfer information from one to another, or simply access one application from another to check a detail with as little disk-swapping, booting, rebooting and forgetting directories as possible.

Integrated software does not, however, offer the same appeal all over the world. Europe is a multi-lingual and multi-cultural environment – in which not only the execution of – but the ideas behind – personal computer software packages are tested to the full. A given package may succeed in the US because it has a 'style' or 'feel' that is comfortable to US end-users, but bomb in Europe precisely because it is 'too American'.

But good ideas cut across all languages and cultures, and succeed world-wide. The spreadsheet, for example, was developed in the US as a 'visible calculator', but was such a universally important productivity tool that it had as big an impact in the EEC as it did in the US.

Integrated software was another international 'good idea', which has hopes of succeeding everywhere, simply because it makes life – and particularly the portion of it that involves using computers – so much easier. Like the wheel, the fountain pen and the automobile, integrated software is a powerful tool which makes people's lives easier and their time more productive.

So although the cosmetics of the software industry may change between European and US markets, the fundamental principles are still the same. Powerful software tools which increase productivity are in big demand and programs which fulfil that demand will sell – no matter what country they are marketed in.

Having established that integrated software is a good idea, it's helpful to look at different ways of implementing that idea. After all, flying was a good idea – but it wasn't until men came down from their hot-air balloons and got into aeroplanes that it really became viable or efficient.

There are three main ways to obtain software integration;

1 Through integrated architecture, which combines all applications in a single package that's loaded in RAM and uses common data formats to allow for almost instantaneous exchange of data between one application and another. Lotus' own Symphony integrated software suite would be included in this category.

2 Through an operating environment – such as Microsoft Windows, Digital Research GEM XM, or the Apple Lisa/Macintosh desktop – which takes existing or specially-configured stand-alone applications packages and forces them to work with one another and exchange data with one another.

3 Through an integrating background program – such as the Perfect Software applications suite and Psion's Xchange system – which takes a series of stand-alone packages developed by one software house and builds some communicating links between them.

Each of these routes has its own advantages and disadvantages, but I should point out that of all the approaches to integration, the first method – that used by Symphony – is the most flexible for the end-user, who is, when all is said and done, the most important element in the equation.

Operating environments can be very good, but they lock you into using programs that run under that environment and make very specific demands on the way software houses code their programs and users use them. With Apple's Macintosh, for instance, the operating environment demands the use of a mouse for much of the input – leaving those who prefer cursor keys out in the cold. (The Macintosh Plus does have cursor keys, but they are more an afterthought than anything else on that machine).

Integrating background programs, although they may allow you to build an integrated suite one brick at a time, also make you do more work to exchange your data – often requiring you to use valuable disk space in buffering data in and out using 'transfer' formats.

Integrated architecture, however, operates entirely in RAM and the mechanics of the common data format are entirely invisible to the user. Symphony, with the right amount of memory, can run on everything from a single disk system to a hard disk with tape streamer backup and built-in micro-to-mainframe communications configurations.

THE FLEXIBILITY OF INTEGRATED SOFTWARE

Over and above any other considerations, the flexibility behind programs using integrated architecture stems from the way in which they can be tailored.

Many integrated applications now offer 'macros' which can learn certain standard keyboard sequences, run their own powerful high-level command languages and can use 'add-in' vertical market applications to tackle specific tasks.

Macros are easy for the novice integrated software user to master. Either by using simple English-like commands, or by putting the micro in 'learn' mode and entering some oft-repeated keystrokes, the program can be 'taught' how to work in a more personalised fashion.

The command language takes this one step further and allows the direct tailoring of the program's appearance and execution with commands which will quickly be familiar to users of both the Basic computer language and the good old English language. This control of a high-level language within the application package itself makes it much more likely that the sophisticated office user can tailor the package to work much more in the way he works.

And finally, there are the 'add-in' applications – vertical market tasks which can be tackled by additional modules within the main integrated software suite. These could come from the original software supplier, a company's own DP department or a specialist third-party software house.

This flexibility is important because if integrated software, or any other type of office productivity tool, is to be useful it must address specific needs and problems.

But what effect is that flexibility going to have in the European market – a market whose needs would seem to be perhaps more diverse than anywhere else in the world? Answering that question requires looking at a bit of history.

The European software market came into existence via the Apple II – which was taken up in Europe more as a serious business tool than as the popular hobbyist machine which pioneered the US home computer business. To make use of that tool, European companies often had to use English-language software – not a great help if you're trying to print-out a database report in French, or a word-processed letter in German. It should come as no surprise, then, that the first really popular piece of software in Europe was the spreadsheet – which dealt mainly in the more international language of numbers and formulae.

But even in spreadsheets, differing currencies and character sets can make the difference between frustration and productivity. So when Lotus entered this market with 1–2–3 (and later Symphony), it included the Lotus International Character Set – or LICS. It enables users to generate English pound signs, German Deutsche marks, Swiss francs and other European currencies.

Developing international versions of applications software is not cheap, nor is it easy. Changes have to be made not only to the character sets and all program menus and commands, but also to all the documentation. And, as anyone who ever bought a Japanese car in the Sixties and struggled with the often unintentionally funny manuals can attest to, many things can get lost in the translation – including a company's credibility.

Software companies cannot, nor should they be seen to, churn out local translations of manuals without paying just as much care and detailed attention to that process as they did in writing the original documentation. No matter how good a program is, no-one's going to get much out of it until they know how to use it.

And with the current size of the integrated software market in Europe, that kind of sensitivity is commercially important. The size is difficult to estimate, but the *Washington Post* suggested recently that Europe alone could be a $1 billion annual market.

Among the players involved in this competitive European integrated software market include Lotus, Ashton-Tate, Psion and Software Products International.

The future prospects are even more rosy. If American growth is anything to go by – with sales of more than 100,000 units of 1–2–3 in Lotus' first nine months on the market – then demand for integrated software will continue to grow.

It should start taking over not only the traditional stand-alone software markets, but also make inroads with users who have never considered computer software easy enough to use or learn.

The development of picture-driven computers and the friendly interface that goes with them have made software accessible to a much wider audience – people who want to get a computer on their desk at noon and be able to do something useful with it by one o'clock. The success of this style of hardware and software such as Lotus 1–2–3 indicate a great potential for friendly, integrated software solutions.

There are three major types of PC users and each is defined by the environment in which they use their software:

1 Large corporate environments in which communications and connection to mainframes is important.

2 Small corporate environments where single-user systems occupy the desk-tops and they very much fit the philosophy of the 'personal' computer.

3 Individual professional users who take off-the-shelf software and make it useful for them.

But in addition to those three sectors – which are somewhat universal – European users have further special needs, including multiple character sets and multi-lingual environments. These are genuine cultural and business needs – where the inclusion of the aforementioned international character sets in packages like Psion's Xchange and Symphony are important in order to satisfy them.

Besides the obvious linguistic and cultural differences, there is the question of challenge. Europeans like to be challenged, and generally seem to approach software with a higher level of sophistication – they don't mind using command languages in designing their own macros.

Companies like Sinclair Research, which helped develop computer and programming literacy in the UK, fuelled this sophistication. Europeans respond positively to the power of command languages and macros and have actively pursued training markets and development of add-in packages.

The time lag between the spread of integrated software in the US and Europe in fact assisted in the success of the product, because it has given time for this RAM price drop to take effect. Europeans have 'jumped' technology before – recently moving straight from mainframes to super-minis, without any of the intervening stages.

Integrated software is ideal for the individual professional to use who, as mentioned before, is more sophisticated and likely to have a background in Basic.

This professional user has been a major force behind the take-up of machines such as Apple's Macintosh. It introduces a software-led market – where people say 'Have you seen MacPaint – I'll have to get a Mac to use it.'

Another surprising development is that the price elasticity of software isn't as great as that of hardware which has fallen dramatically in price in recent years. Software has been pushing that hardware to its limits – but now those limits have been moved with developments like the 512K Macintosh, the Compaq Deskpro 386 and popularity of multi-user, multi-tasking systems.

Flexible integrated software also means a changed role for the DP manager – who had until recently been chiefly characterised as the officious person who grudgingly gave people access to dumb terminals to get onto the mainframe. Integrated software can provide a shift in purpose for DP managers and means they can now be called in as internal computer consultants who have got to protect the security of company data, ensure that proper protocols are available and observed, data is used properly and the company's investment is protected.

To help you in your choice of integrated software, I have included the following reviews of recent integrated software products, which will provide criteria by which these and other packages like them can be judged. The packages themselves may well have been updated and revised by the time you read this – it is provided only as a rough comparative guide.

ELECTRIC DESK

Integrated software has been something of a 'flavour of the month' for the past couple of years. Symphony and Framework have been widely applauded by the computer press, although sales have not matched up to either Lotus or Ashton-Tate's original expectations.

Unfortunately, integrated software is also traditionally (if anything introduced within the last few years can be said to have any traditions) an expensive proposition. So you would think there could well be a good market for less expensive integrated products. If you did, you would have come to the same conclusion as the American Alpha Software company – which was one of the first companies to release a sub-£300 application in the UK in the form of its Electric Desk package.

Features

Electric Desk includes a database, word-processor, spreadsheet and communications package. The only one of the 'big-five' applications missing is a business graphics system (which Alpha considered an unnecessary luxury you probably wouldn't use). And within each of those applications you can open up as many 'services' (a service is a spreadsheet, document, database file or communications set-up) as the memory of your machine can hold.

Because all of your work is held in memory, you can swap between one service and another with just a few keystrokes. There are no 'windows' in the conventional sense, although a split screen serves much the same purpose (Alpha Software says that it couldn't see many situations when it would be useful to have more than two windows – i.e. you can't really concentrate on more than two things at once).

One aspect in which this split-screen approach is more useful than the conventional windowing approach is where the HELP menus are concerned. With most help menus – even context-sensitive ones – you have to write down, or somehow remember, what the help menu says because you can't see the thing you need help about and the help menu itself at the same time. The split-screen context-sensitive help facility in Electric Desk gets round this problem.

Documentation

There's a fine line between user-friendliness/simplicity and inadequacy, particularly when it comes to software documentation. It's hard to tell which side of the fine line Electric Desk's documentation falls on.

The manual is broken up by tabbed dividers into sections on each of the individual packages within the system and a chapter dealing with the overall 'work environment'. There is everything you need to know to do most common tasks with each of the packages, provided you're not trying to establish a huge, complex database or a particularly wide-ranging spreadsheet.

There's 45 pages devoted to using the word-processor, 69 pages on the database, 60 pages on the spreadsheet and a mere 18 pages on the communications service (much of which deals with American communications systems that are largely irrelevant to UK users).

In use

Like most low-priced integrated packages, Electric Desk is pretty easy to use. Most of the applications can be operated without even so much as a passing look at the manual.

Word-processor

The word-processor is a simple full-screen type with on-screen automatic reformatting of text, 'reminder' menus at the top of the screen and a line showing tabs and statistics at the bottom of the screen.

On-screen underlining, bold, italics and Roman typefaces are supported, margins can be changed easily and pasting and cutting is simple. All this is menu-driven. There are no macros, or embedded formatting directly from the keyboard. To embed a command, you must select the 'embedded commands' option from the menu presented by hitting the F–8 'document commands' key.

This menu-driven approach carries through for most of the other functions in the word-processor. But if you're a beginner, that's probably a blessing, as having to learn lots of key-commands right off would be confusing.

One other thing I liked about the word-processor was the print-spooling facility, which worked quickly and effectively. On most print-spooling mechanisms in integrated packages, the type-ahead buffers slow right down and the machine keeps having to jump between the disk, the keyboard and the screen in its I/O handling

– but with Electric Desk, I found the package could quite easily keep up with my typing speed.

Database

The database application is the most complicated in the package and thus the most difficult to comment on in detail. From the limited time I had to look at the database, it seemed quite complete, although perhaps not as 'friendly' as the other three (it was the only application which sent me running to the manual).

Spreadsheet

All the regular spreadsheet functions are in the Electric Desk spreadsheet, although with one odd difference; rows and columns are both accessed by number. So instead of the spreadsheet starting at A1, it starts at a cell reference called R1C1 (Row 1, Column 1). This difference is relatively easy to get used to, however, and the spreadsheet is otherwise as menu-driven and easy to use as the word-processor.

Communications

The communications package supported all the common baud rates and was successfully used with Prestel (though only the 300/300 band text version of the service), One-to-One and for transferring information between micros. The menu-driven approach helped again here and made the application useable without even so much as a glance at the manual.

Verdict

Electric Desk is a good all-round easy-to-use integrated package at about half the cost of most integrated software suites. While it doesn't have all the fancy graphics features of a Symphony or a Framework, it isn't anywhere near as memory-hungry and will run without a memory expansion card. For serious home users, small offices or professionals, Electric Desk can be considered something of a bargain.

PSION XCHANGE

The packages which make up this suite are known individually as Abacus, Quill, Archive and Easel. They are also known collectively as Xchange.

The rationale for this bit of software re-nomenclature is that while you can never see two of the applications running on screen at once, you can easily swap between them – thus 'exchanging' one task for another. Quill is a word-processor, Abacus a spreadsheet, Archive a database and Easel a business graphics system.

Psion is an interesting example of a company which has taken the up-market approach to developing application software – it started down and is working its way up. Psion is marketing Xchange as part-competitor to the Symphony/Framework family of integrated products.

Psion, however, sees Xchange as having the best of both worlds. The packages are actually modular applications which feature the ability to exchange data between them – where it's logical.

This, claims Psion, increases appeal to those who require only a couple of packages – say a database and word-processor, or a database and spreadsheet combination. This design philosophy also allows the packages modest hardware requirements.

Users won't be forced into buying expensive RAM upgrades or hard disks. It will, if you like, provide an intermediate technology between the full-scale integration of something like Symphony and the very separate integrating approach of packages such as Smart's software suite.

SPI'S OPEN ACCESS

This was one of the first so-called integrated packages on the UK scene. It's really a collection of separate packages accessible from a front end 'options' menu – just one step away from the bundled suite approach.

Minimum system requirements involve at least 192K and a pair of standard IBM floppy disk drives. Optimum benefit requires 640K, colour graphics board and a Winchester drive. It is possible, however, to use the system with relative ease from the standard floppy disk set-up, albeit in a truncated form. You could load a couple of the more intensively-used packages – say the spreadsheet and the database, onto one disk and use a common data disk. With some of the more integrated products this sort of option is far less attractive.

Real windowing is absent – you can't have more than two applications displayed in windows on the screen. Windows are provided to display file directories and command key help.

Word-processor

This is very good. A single file of about 5000 words can be worked on (with a 256K system). There is no word counter, but it does just about everything else. The block move is especially easy to use.

Information manager

It's a relational database system. You can have up to five files sharing information and being reported on together. The system utilises a sophisticated, English-like query language.

Spreadsheet

Features all the usual spreadsheet functions with the interesting addition of goal seeking. In a normal spreadsheet, of course, you set up a series of projected costs and incomings to see how dire the financial situation is going to be over a certain time frame.

Goal-seeking allows you to reverse the process. You can set up a profit or sales target and see just how hopeless it's going to be to reach it.

Graphics

The graphics package is only compromised by the difficult data transference procedures. However, its ability to create pretty three dimensional graphs and display a series of graphs on the screen at a time make up for this drawback.

Time manager

This is a simple diary/daybook application which allows you to store reminders and plan upcoming events on the PC. For myself, however, I've often thought that computer-based diary systems are pretty useless. Some things are still better when left to pen and paper. Given the lack of application windowing, I wouldn't place too much store on this module. The really great thing about a book diary is its portability, the great thing about a Winchester disk is its lack thereof. Time Manager makes a good toy.

Communications

Like most of the integrated packages, communications is viewed as very important. Unfortunately, most also set great store on the Hayes Smart Modem as the US standard – still, all the usual comms facilities are well supported on this.

In use

The data transfer aspects are not the most sophisticated, but at least there is a commonality of application structure and commands. There are three ways of transferring information. The Context method allows you to move the data with you as you go from package to package.

A more conventional method involves writing the information to a SIF (Standard Interface File) and then bringing it back again. You can also write data to an ASCII file. The variety of methods says something about the ease of integration – obviously, each method has advantages in a specific transfer context, which in turn means that there are situations in which any one of them is inadequate.

This is unfortunate as the advantage of integration relates directly to how easily and unproblematical the transfer procedure is.

Verdict

Open Access bundles some good applications together and attempts to provide the illusion of integration by providing some transfer procedures and a front-end from which you can load each of the packages in turn.

FRAMEWORK II

Framework II is the latest version of Ashton-Tate's popular and good-looking integrated software offering. It incorporates the usual database, spreadsheet and word-processing functions – along with business graphics, communications and import/export software.

It does support the Lotus-Intel-Microsoft expanded memory specification, but also uses 'virtual memory' – so that if you run out of RAM memory in which to store your information, it will be 'spooled' to the disk drive or hard disk. This means that files are no longer restricted to RAM size.

The impressive 'outlining' facilities which impressed so many reviewers in the first edition of Framework are back in Framework II – with the important difference that Telecommunications frames can now be part of the 'frame-within-a-frame' outlining structure.

'Unrelated' frames (database, spreadsheet and graphics frames, for example) can thus be 'linked' within a single file. Information can also be easily 'copied' between frames on-screen and a large number of frames can be viewed at once.

Using the 'zoom' facility, you can concentrate on one frame at a time – while still having a large number immediately available at once across a range of applications.

Commands are entered either via 'CTRL' commands or via a 'pull-down' menu called up by the INSERT key. Functions – such as ZOOM, COPY, MOVE and HELP – are all accessed via the ten IBM PC function keys.

As in the original version of the program, programmable keyboard 'macros' are also provided using the Framework 'FRED' programming language. With improved documentation and added commands, the language is more powerful and much easier to use.

There are a few nice additions to the word-processor as well – a contents section has been added, auto page-numbering is a new feature and a quick word-count command makes the application perfect for deadline-driven writers.

In summary, the things to look for in a good integrated software package are:

● Common commands for each application – to cut down learning time and encourage use of the full package.

● The fullest possible functionality in each of the applications which make up the suite – they are often quite unbalanced with, for example, a great spreadsheet and a lousy word-processor.

● Virtual memory operation – you never want to be limited by the size of your computer's memory. Packages which allow you to split documents between RAM and disk space (i.e. using virtual memory) get round this problem.

● Windowing – it may not always be necessary to see several files or documents on-screen at once, but having the facility to do so can make a great difference in a package's flexibility.

● Speed – the effort which goes into making more and more functionality available within an integrated package can often sacrifice the speed you have come to expect in stand-alone software. Check the speed of operation on your PC before you buy.

● Data interchange – integrated packages don't always offer 'two-way' data exchange. It's relatively easy, for example, to allow database and spreadsheet information to be added to a word-processed document. But it is often far more difficult to send data from a spreadsheet directly to a database.

● Documentation – perhaps more than any other type of software, integrated packages require that you really do have full and complete background information on how you use each of the 'modules' within the suite.

Chapter Nine

Inter-office communications

You should by now have a pretty good idea of how your PC can be used to put together reports and figures for both on-paper and 'on-line' use by people in your own office, but what about sending paperless information to people outside your office or your company?

PAPERLESS POPULARITY

There's no doubt that this option is a popular one among users in many countries – on both sides of the great Atlantic divide.

Computer-to-computer communications is probably the fastest rising of any new applications for microcomputers.

A recent study in the United Kingdom suggested that top executives are often far more concerned with getting information from the company's on-line database than they are in running spreadsheet analyses or their own databases.

The survey, conducted jointly by the British Department of Trade and Industry and the London-based EOSYS consultancy service, polled 350 top UK companies about their uses of computer equipment and found that communications was far more important than most manufacturers have suggested.

The UK survey is only one of a growing number of indicators about how important computer-based communications is becoming. Sales of internal and external 'modems' have long been healthy in the US and have recently started to pick up in Europe – particularly the internal variety. Although such devices have long been available in the U.S., local government telephone regulations have slowed the approval of such devices in the U.K. and Europe.

CUTTING COSTS

Growing numbers of users are realising that their work can be conducted more efficiently and with greater speed if they don't have to allow half a day or, even, half a month for their information to travel by messenger or post to some other part of the world. Investment in a good modem and communications system could considerably cut down your costs on both courier and FAX services.

The power to achieve widespread distribution of computer communications services has existed for some time but has been held back by a general public ignorance of what computer communications can do for computer users.

THE BIG FOUR

There are essentially four major areas of application for computer-to-computer communications: local area networks (LANs); electronic mail; electronic telexing; and public access databases (also known as VANs or value-added networks). Two of these applications – electronic mail and electronic telexing – seem to attract the most attention from businesses, as they provide immediate utility.

Looking at lans

The first level of communication is local area networking, which allows 'clusters' of computers to share information – as well as computer add-ons such as disk drives, printers or 'hard disks'. The usual method of operating networks involves having a 'network manager' and training network users to familiarise themselves with a special set of new network commands.

Recent advances in networks, however, have meant that they can often be operated as simple extensions to your PC's MS-DOS operating system. There are also network 'overlays' – such as the picture-based Torus Icon system – which allow you to issue network commands via a mouse.

Enterprising E–mail

But networks only affect computers that are physically hooked up to the network. Electronic mail, on the other hand, will have a large impact on the way computers talk to one another around the world.

Electronic mail is a system which allows computer users to send information to each other via a central computer. Users 'dial up' the central computer over the phone line using a modem, and send 'addressed' information to the central computer, where it is stored in a specific area for collection by the recipient – who sees the message when he or she next phones up the central computer.

American business computer users have a wide choice of such services, including Easylink, The Source and Compuserve. In the UK, it is the recently-privatised British Telecom's Telecom Gold system that leads the way in electronic mail communications. It claims up to 22,000 users and offers local access calls to the system from 96 per cent of the telephones in the UK.

The biggest problem with electronic mail, however, is that there are a growing number of electronic mail services – and subscribers to one service often can't send messages to subscribers of another.

People who use the British One-to-One service (an independently-run alternative to Telecom Gold that also offers electronic mail, electronic telexing, radio-paging and a 24-hour help-line), for example, cannot easily send electronic mail messages to US Compuserve users. Subscribers also cannot easily send electronic messages to people who don't have computers.

Talking about telex

And that's where electronic telex systems come in. Electronic telex systems allow you to prepare information electronically using a computer's word-processor, and then send that information over the telephone to a central computer – which is, in turn, linked into the worldwide telex system. The electronic telex is received at the central computer and then sent out over the phone line to any standard telex machine throughout the world.

Such a service eliminates the problem of communicating with non-subscribers, and often gives you a full send/receive telex system into the bargain. Electronic mail and telex systems are thus often sold together. The only drawback of these systems over conventional telexes is that you only know when you've got a telex if you actually phone up the system to check.

One way around the telex-checking problem is to buy dedicated telex hardware for your computer. A number of companies offer a 'telex manager' system which will turn a standard PC into a full-blown constantly-running telex terminal. Such a system is usually added to the PC via a 'serial card' and provides software for constant monitoring of the telex line for incoming messages, 'queuing' of outgoing telexes, automatic 'retries' when a telex number is busy and the sending of word-processed documents as telexes.

Getting into vans

The other big communications growth area is in the development of VANs or Value Added Networks, which offer vast amounts of information easily accessed through a conventional phone, a computer and a modem.

In addition to government and phone-company-run information

services such as Britain's Prestel viewdata system, Canada's Telidon, Japan's Captain and the French Teletel, there is also a movement towards development of specialised news and business services.

The two big guns in this information sweepstakes in the US are Compuserve and The Source, which both offer extensive libraries of 'on-line' information on a huge variety of subjects. In Europe, one of the leaders in these private news services is Datasolve – an arm of the giant British Thorn-EMI electronics company. Its World Reporter and World Exporter services offer a vast range of daily information, including full daily transcripts of major newspapers such as the *Financial Times*, *Asashi Shibum*, the *New York Times*, *Tass*, the *Economist* and the *Guardian*.

STARTING SMALL

The place you're likely to start in sending messages between two computers is at the network level. Networks can be a complex business, however, and it's well worth looking at how a few other companies have gone about the business of getting them to work before investing in one yourself.

The best way to develop a PC application is to learn from the mistakes of others – and there never seems to be a short supply of them.

ASSESS FIRST

In an informal survey of corporate PC users in 1985, large firms such as ICI and British Aerospace were found to be busy assessing a variety of PC-based local area network systems for use in their offices. The biggest problem most of them faced was integrating a PC-based system into an environment largely dominated by mini and mainframe computers.

British Aerospace (BA), for example, hedged its bets on all communications fronts. The corporation's Stevenage headquarters comprises some 32 different buildings in a site three-quarters of a mile long and one-quarter of a mile wide. This has meant that it needed both 'site networks' to link all the buildings and 'building networks' for more local communications.

The site network is provided by a broad-band system which runs the length of the site (and which was purpose-built into the site when it was designed), while building networks comprise a whole range of systems including Ethernet, Polynet and various other PC networks. By providing this choice of links, the company is very definitely keeping its options open.

BA uses PCs, with the odd 286 machine starting to make an appearance these days. The site network uses the broad-band cabling, although access from the PCs to the mainframe is also conducted via the broadband system.

Corporate clusters

Systems specialists for the company say, however, that it spent a good deal of time trying to build some form of communications standard from all this. Those evaluations pointed to a need for more 'cluster systems' – where, for example, a 286 or 386 machine could act as main file server for a small office – instead of having to share a larger file server with a bigger group of people.

This is particularly interesting to the many engineers who work on the site – and for whom the daily exchange of data is important. They will probably be among the first to move to 'cluster-based' systems which use large file-servers and offer excellent local data-exchange facilities.

SMALL NETS, BIG PROBLEMS

Smaller offices – such as the UK headquarters of Ashton-Tate (the purveyors of dBase and Framework software) – have already spent some time coming to grips with these kinds of problems. Ashton-Tate's two-year old office network has provided it with a battery of cautionary tales for network users.

The Ashton-Tate system is used primarily as a way of offering users a wide choice of peripherals, while saving money on the number of such devices it has to buy. Documents, for example, can be printed by anyone on the network using one of six different printers – including letter-quality and high-speed dot-matrix types. But the network allows the company to maintain a one-to-four ratio of printers to workstations – as well as fewer hard-disk storage systems.

The 3-COM-based network started out with only four terminals and has grown to a 25-station system which includes PCs, XTs and one Altos with a 40-Megabyte hard disk. Anyone managing such a network is advised to pay a great deal of attention to detail in developing the network.

GET PHYSICAL

The experiences of Ashton-Tate and others suggest that the security of cable-laying is also of paramount concern, as intermittent faults on the network's cable line can play havoc with the system. Other than the lessons of experience, it is also recommended that network managers know exactly how the system works before they use it.

This may sound all too obvious, but Ashton-Tate relates the tale of how its hard-disk space kept being gobbled up by 'print-spooling' requests which were never deleted once the printing had taken place. The problem was particularly acute, as Ashton-Tate relies on the hard-disk component of the network as a file-server and electronic mail system. The solution was to write an 'autoexec' file which deletes all the print-spool files every week-end – but the company didn't arrive at that solution until it had been using the system for a while.

TAKE TIME

It's also a good idea for network managers to take a hard look at how people in their offices work. Network-based internal electronic mail systems, for example, don't work unless everyone uses them. An office, for example, which works half the time with paper-based memos and half with electronic messages is bound to get confused.

You should also not limit your choice of operating systems for a networked or multi-user environment. Although you may be used to MS-DOS, if you have a heavy load of networked applications, it may be well worth also looking at Xenix (the MS-DOS version of the Unix multi-user operating system).

E-MAIL AND YOU

At some point, however, you and your colleagues will have to stop taking in each other's electronic laundry and start communicating with the outside world – and it's at this point that you should consider the benefits of a good electronic mail system.

Unfortunately before you start any communicating on the phone line, you will have to spend some money. There are two – possibly three – things that you'll have to get: a modem, some communications software and (if you don't already have one) an expansion card with an RS–232 communications card in it. The last item won't be needed if you get an internal modem that plugs into your PC's on-board expansion slot area.

In terms of what the modem should look like, it doesn't matter desperately as long as it's made by a reputable company and conforms to the defacto 'Hayes' standard for modems. Hayes is a US company which had the foresight to pioneer internal modems for the Apple II and IBM PC machines in the late seventies and early eighties.

The company's early entry into the market (combined with a high-quality product) ensured that US software houses specialising in communications software took the Hayes modem into account when developing their packages.

As a result, almost all the US communications packages – and a number of integrated software suites – take the Hayes internal modem as the IBM PC communications hardware standard. And, if you're lucky enough to have a Hayes modem, you can auto-dial, auto-answer and even arrange 'alarm' calls using popular communications software. So, armed with a Hayes-type modem and some communications software, you're ready to tackle sending electronic messages.

The postal system of the future

Although it's called electronic mail (or 'E-mail'), electronic message-sending services probably have more in common with the telex system than with the postal system. And in many ways, there are parallels to the way the systems will be used. The key to understanding electronic mail is to realise that, like Telex, E-mail is comprised of private, non-standard closed systems.

You can't universally stick a 'stamp' onto a piece of electronic mail and have it delivered anywhere in the world. Both the sender and receiver must be members of the same electronic mail service in order for the system to work (just as companies communicating by telex could only do so when both parties have telex machines).

Given those limitations, electronic mail is still powerful. It's the quickest way to get computer-generated text from one person to another in a big hurry and provides the recipient with the greatest flexibility in handling the message (i.e. printing it out, saving it to disk, modifying it in a word-processor, or sending it on elsewhere when they are finished with it).

Electronic mail is operated by using a computer and its storage system as a combined mailbox/letter-box and sorting house. The electronic mail computer runs a program which allows it to talk to your computer by phone. So when you call up the E-mail computer, it answers the phone and prepares to either deliver mail that's waiting for you, or take in the mail you want to deliver to someone else.

So you can see that electronic mail is really nothing more than creative sharing of a central computer – where the computer acts as postbox, sorting office and postman. But how extensive that mail system is depends largely on the computer that's running it. The best advice I can give on electronic mail is that either you make sure that everyone with whom you do most of your business is registered on the same mail system as you, or that you look at mail systems with telex links.

E-mail and telex

A good number of popular E-mail systems these days also include links into the worldwide telex networks – for both sending and receiving telexes. Beware, however, that there are limitations to this type of service and you should keep them in mind when looking at your communications alternatives.

The major limitation is that you often only find out that you've got a telex when you take the time to 'log-on' to your electronic mail service to pick it up. There's little point in having an urgent messaging medium, such as telex, if you don't keep a close eye on it.

There are, of course, ways round this problem. Either you can invest in a dedicated computer-based telex system such as Braid Systems's popular Telex Manager software/hardware package, or you can sign on to one of the E-mail services that issues you with a 'bleeper' that goes off every time there's a telex.

The other feature to watch for in E-mail telex systems is how messages look when they reach you. As the international telex standard was designed some years ago (it grew out of the Morse code telegraphy systems of the 18th century), it supports only upper-case letters and you may thus find it hard to incorporate telex-generated messages directly into a document.

THE VAN LIBRARY

Recent advances in micro-based information and communications services suggests that the corporate library might soon be superseded by the on-line database. But like many other technology advancements, the concept still has to be thought through before you start giving notice to the corporate librarian.

The ability of on-line information services such as Datasolve's 'World Reporter' and the recently-launched 'Knowledge Index' to provide instant 'keyword searches' of a variety of major daily, weekly and monthly publications might make you think that the vast number of newspaper and magazine clippings libraries will, in many cases, be unnecessary.

If, for example, you were writing a report about the tractor-purchase market among farmers in the US Mid-West – using material from the *Financial Times* – you would normally have to thumb through the cross-referenced sections of many dog-eared and fading pink clippings to find what you want.

On a service such as World Reporter, you would just enter the FT database and ask it to search for the words 'tractor' and 'US Mid-West' – and it would pull out all the articles in a specified period which contained those words. Be warned, however, that on-line databases are very fussy creatures and you need to spend a good deal of time planning an on-line inquiry before you wade into making it.

THE END OF MICRO-MAINFRAME COLD WAR

Communications software will also help you end the computer industry's cold war between micros and mainframes. Like two competing ideologies, micro and mainframe business computer systems have for years been reluctant to 'talk' to one another.

The micro was defined by no less a company than IBM as the 'Personal Computer' which could be operated by executives from their desks, while the mainframe was far more of a communal efficiency tool which had its information and operation managed by the ubiquitous data processing manager. Free enterprise versus centralised bureaucracy, you might say.

But like the real world cold war, the two ideologies involved in this electronic battle are now seeking a way to accommodate and even complement one another. This peaceful, and even helpful, co-existence is being made possible by systems which allow effective communication between the mainframe and the micro.

Micro-to-mainframe communications systems extend the life of the mainframe systems by letting micro users access them and enhance the power of micros by allowing those micros quick access to the wide range of information held on a mainframe. Such systems also minimise the need for information duplication between the two systems. Software development to facilitate these links, however, is a slow and evolving process.

Strategy in selecting your micro-mainframe link is all-important, as exchanging information between the micro and mainframe systems is not an easy task. There are at least three ways to do it;

1 Making the micro 'emulate' a mainframe. Although this is the simplest and often cheapest solution to the communications problem, it is the least sophisticated. There are many programs which will allow a variety of personal computers to dial-up mainframe computers and act as terminals to those computers. But in order to do so, the person at the micro end must be familiar with the command language of the mainframe.

And if you don't know your way round a mainframe database, your chances of finding the information you want are about as good as those of finding a needle in the proverbial haystack. In addition, information captured by the micro in 'terminal emulation mode' will not necessarily be in a form that the micro's applications software can use and is thus of limited use. This emulation can be made 'asynchronously' by hooking the micro up to a telephone and getting it to 'dial-up' the mainframe or by putting extra hardware into both the mainframe and micro systems and going for a dedicated 'synchronous' system that forms a private exchange within the company.

2 Making the mainframe act more like a micro. There are severe limitations to this option, as the nature of the beasts is so very different. All you can really do is install a program on the mainframe that answers calls from micros in a far more 'friendly' and easy-to-use fashion than those received in terminal emulation mode. This also usually means that a special package must be used at the micro end to use the link to the mainframe. But this option usually requires the use of terminal-style micros, such as IBM's 3270 series.

3 A combination of the previous two options. This involves the development of 'translation' programs which let micro users make use of mainframe data by accessing it through programs they are familiar with and which at the other end translate those micro-style commands into something the mainframe can understand and act on quickly and efficiently.

This form of communication makes primary use of the first link-up option, although you can get products that also align it with the third – packages such as Sterling Software's Micro Answer, a micro-to-mainframe communications system that allows micro users of popular micro software like Lotus 1–2–3 and Symphony to pull down data that will be usable and understandable to either of those products.

OF COURSE, YOU CAN ALWAYS BUY . . .

There is – as you might imagine – an alternative to spending a great deal of time getting your own collection of PC communications applications together.

You can now buy – from Compaq and a number of companies with which it has agreements in the US (sorry, at the time of writing it's not yet available in the rest of the world) – the Telecompaq, a dedicated communications computer with full IBM compatibility, all the extra Compaq features you've come to expect from them, as well as a built-in modem, telephone, auto-dialler and some excellent multi-tasking communications software. If you live in an area where you can get one of these machines – and you're serious about communications – then it's well worth a look.

Chapter Ten

Presentations, graphics and mice

You may not be able to judge a book by its cover, but computer users have long judged computer programs by the way they look. The importance of presentation in business computer software led the business microcomputer industry to turn to graphics in a big way in the early 1980s.

The first attempts to bring computer graphics to bear on making business computer software easier and more effective to use were made by Xerox with its Xerox Star range of computers. But the real breakthrough for computer graphics in business came with the release of Apple's Lisa computer in late 1982. For the first time, computer users could issue commands to the machine via pictures.

The Lisa was, unfortunately, a very expensive machine – even among the large corporate clients who were expected to use it. It cost about $10,000 US from launch – and never got significantly cheaper (compared to the rest of the business computer market) because it was so expensive to start with. And because it made so much use of graphics (as well as a then-unknown alternative input device known as a mouse), very few existing computer programs could be easily converted for use with the machine.

GRAPHICS GET NOTICED

If the Lisa didn't sell well (which even Apple admits was the state of affairs when it finally withdrew the machine in 1985), it did both capture the imagination of the general public and create a revolution in microcomputer software and hardware design. Business users, for the first time, started to sit up and take notice of computer graphics and realise how useful they could be in making highly complex software accessible to many more business information processing executives.

Many programmers then started to work on developing Lisa-style touches to their software. Spreadsheet giant Visicorp announced that it had started work on its 'VisiON' Lisa-style system and microcomputer systems houses Microsoft and Digital Research indicated they too would be working on such systems. Lotus then released its revolutionary 1–2–3 spreadsheet with graphics built-in and Apple unveiled its Macintosh.

Of the two, the release of 1–2–3 had the most immediate effect on the production of business graphics using PCs. It allowed users to produce:

● Line graphs – often used to show a value (or a number of values) changing over time.

● Bar graphs – best for comparing the same value for different items.

● Pie charts – a well-known method of demonstrating how parts of a whole are distributed.

● Stacked bar charts – a clear way of showing several values for several items.

● X–Y graphs – which show a simple relationship between two changing graphs.

While users bought 1–2–3 in droves and took a cautious look at the ideas behind the Mac (although not as many business users as Apple would have initially liked actually took the plunge), a host of PC-based imitators soon appeared for both Lotus and the Mac – mainly with 'Mac-like' products for the IBM. The first of these to be released was Digital Research's GEM (Graphics Environment Manager) system, which offered a 'Paint' program, word-processor, a 'draw' package and some business graphics preparation software.

Not to be outdone, Microsoft moved into the Mac-style market late in 1985 with its long-awaited Windows system – which also offered both writing and painting software that was heavily reliant on graphics. To give you an idea of how such a graphic environment can be used, I'll take a detailed look here at the operation of GEM (Windows – more a multi-tasking environment with graphics than a pure graphics environment – is discussed in the next chapter).

The thing that will make or break GEM is how necessary it is. There is a school of thought which suggests that GEM and other graphically-defined interfaces have a limited appeal and that they are only part of a current fad in the software industry. This line of reasoning also suggests that users may grow to resent the software's 'hand-holding' approach once they've been using it for six months.

Proponents of this view also say that 'you can't introduce a graphics standard for a product which already has five million users quite happily using it without one'. They also worry that both the Digital Research offering and the Microsoft product will be superseded by an upcoming IBM product.

Although I can't say I agree with this approach, I do think that both GEM and Windows have to build up a big software base quickly – with quality that rivals that of similar Macintosh and non-graphic PC products. For if there is no new software to constantly add to the range of possible applications within GEM, then the growth of the GEM market could be severely stunted.

If there is one major advantage offered by GEM's major competitor, Microsoft Windows, it would have to be the latter's sophisticated multi-tasking and memory management system – which allows a number of applications to be running in memory at the same time. DR's updated GEM XM system goes some way to solving that problem, but that's another story.

Of course, the only way that you get reasonable applications running concurrently in a graphics-based system that's already quite memory-hungry is by adding more RAM to your system – and Microsoft has endorsed the Lotus-Intel-Microsoft (LIM) specification to do so. But according to Digital Research, GEM offers more in the way of multi-tasking and concurrency by not going the Above-board route.

DR has plumped for AST's RAMpage! board – which operates as a 'superset' of the Intel/Lotus specification – in conjunction with its own new version of Concurrent DOS, which for the first time allows you to run both CP/M AND MS–DOS applications concurrently.

The AST scheme allows memory expansion through up to four 2 Mb memory expansion boards fitted inside the PC – thus going far beyond the machine's previous 640K RAM limit.

The RAMpage! system hopes to set a further memory standard by being fully compatible with the LIM specification – so that all software written to take advantage of the extra memory in the Lotus/ Intel Above-board will also be able to use that extra RAM, and more, in the AST offering.

The RAMpage! software driver is written so that it 'swaps' 16K pages of applications resident in RAMpage! memory in and out of the PC's normal address range using 64K expanded memory address registers, thus allowing a window onto up to 1 Mb of expanded memory at a time.

In fact, GEM is much more the kind of product that will be better to use as more powerful PCs become cheaper and more widely available. On a standard disk-based IBM PC, for example, GEM is frustratingly slow, constantly accessing the floppies and demanding disk swapping and very hungry on memory.

But if you had a Compaq Deskpro 386 – which includes built-in ways of handling the LIM specification with on-board extended memory – the software would run several times faster than even the original Apple Mac's own desktop system from which GEM is derived.

Even moving to an 80286-based machine like the Deskpro 286 and transferring the software from disk to hard disk makes a very big difference. With the increased processor speed and the expanded (and speeded-up) storage facilities, GEM really begins to shine. Add the AST RAMpage board, along with Digital Research's Concurrent DOS XM system – which allows you to run numerous applications at once in its up-to 8 Mb of RAM space – and then you really have a system that beats most other non-PC graphics options.

SOFTWARE NEEDED

Software development under new environments such as GEM is the key to their success. To give you an idea of exactly what kind of software is available to achieve that success, I looked at a couple of GEM applications: GEM Wordchart and Gem Graph.

GEM Wordchart

The program opens with a divided screen and a series of pull-down menus. In an area occupying about the left fifth of the screen, you see a series of boxed icons which allow you to select the type, size and style you're going to use, what type of 'bullets' you're going to use to highlight on-screen 'points' and whether you want the text right, left or centre justified. The main portion of the screen is given over to your 'chart-creation' area, with a small 'ruler' at the top showing your left and right margins.

The default setting for Wordchart is with a 'title bar' across the top and a series of highlighted 'points' in the indented lines beneath.

You can't really get a good grasp of what a program like Wordchart can actually do until you start using it. When combined with DR's built-in GEM 'output' software, you can run a whole presentation from your PC (perhaps combined with a large video screen or monitor) by 'stacking' Wordchart, Graph and GEM Draw images one after another so that each time you press the mouse button, you see a new image on screen.

GEM Graph

GEM Graph is a more conventional piece of business graphics software, but again offers Macintosh-like ease-of-use and high-quality graphics within the PC environment. Unlike some other business graphics software – which requires that you import data from spreadsheets, or that you restrict yourself to very 'primary' data input with the graphic system itself – GEM Graph actually operates within two layered 'windows' offering spreadsheet-style direct input or importing from other spreadsheets.

When you boot-up GEM Graph, you'll see what looks to be an ordinary spreadsheet. In fact, you'll see a very large spreadsheet – starting at A1 and extending to NK340 (in excess of 100,000 cells) – into which you can either import data from any spreadsheet (such as Lotus 1–2–3, Supercalc or Visicalc) in which data can be stored in Data Interchange Format (DIF) or enter data yourself.

Do not, however, be fooled into thinking that GEM Graph is any replacement for a spreadsheet – it isn't. It can only handle text and numeric data (i.e. labels and numbers) and has no powers to interpret equations. Any real spreadsheet work or planning – barring a quick graph 'knocked out' with a small amount of data – will still have to be conducted using a proper spreadsheet.

But once you've done your spreadsheet, GEM Graph does have some really unique ways of displaying information for you. You can, for example, do statistical map charts with GEM Graph – perhaps showing the sales results for each subsidiary office in Europe next to its appropriate capital city.

And pictures can also become elements of a bar graph. If you wanted to do a bar graph showing the number of men using after-shave in a given year, you could have each 'bar' of the bar chart being comprised of a series of little men – one stacked on top of another.

Probably the best facility of all, however, is the ability to incorporate GEM Graph business graphics with other GEM applications, so that a business graph can be combined with pictures from GEM Draw and GEM Paint.

COMPETITION

Overall, GEM is a well-designed and thoroughly enjoyable windowing environment for the IBM PC – and there is every indication it will become more enjoyable to use as hardware expansion opportunities for the PC increase.

Aside from Microsoft Windows, the other two windowing systems you may hear compared to GEM both begin with a 'T'; IBM's TopView and Epson's Taxi system. In fact, both are designed for radically different jobs – but they both offer windowing and both tend to be compared to GEM.

I'll deal with IBM's offering first, as it is likely to be the most widely-available alternative. TopView is a concurrent windowing system designed by IBM to improve ease of use on its PC, as well as allow users access to more than one piece of software at once.

TopView can be operated by a mouse and does allow you to move applications around the screen within windowed areas. But it makes no attempt to provide a 'graphic interface', does not use icons and does not make use of specially-written applications software (save that software which ensures it is with TopView's 'legal' memory areas).

TopView allows you to switch between standard PC applications – such as Wordstar and dBase II – with a keystroke or two. And it allows you to see these applications together on-screen in separate sized windows. Beyond that, however, TopView doesn't have much in common with GEM and really doesn't belong in a comparison with it.

Taxi, however, is a different story. Epson's simple and clean graphics interface for the IBM PC was first released as a piece of proprietary 'bundled' software on the Epson QX–16 – but the well-known Japanese printer-manufacturer soon realised there was a good deal more money to be made by offering the system for use on all PC-type machines.

Taxi was designed and developed by Epson in the UK and thus doesn't have any of the idiosyncrasies sometimes associated with software from Japanese companies. Like GEM, Taxi offers a graphics-based desktop environment which allows you to transfer files and maintain your hard disk simply by moving icons about the screen. But, unlike the DR offering, Taxi doesn't rely on purpose-built applications to use its mouse and 'pop-up' (as opposed to pull-down) menus.

By using a simple installation procedure, menus and mouse cursor control can be added to existing PC applications such as Lotus 1–2–3, Wordstar and Supercalc. 'Pop-in' accessories (ie. calculator, notepad and clock-calendar) can also be made available within existing applications via Taxi's menus. It must be said, however, that Taxi is more of a 'halfway house' between the full

Mac-style operation of GEM and the simple task-switching of TopView – and it has not been a widespread success.

Put another way, Taxi is a useful utility for making existing applications easier to use, while GEM (and Microsoft Windows) are out to establish a whole new set of graphics-based standards around which entirely new applications are to be developed.

Chapter Eleven

Putting it all together

When you have reached a decision about the types of applications you will be adding or using with your PC, you will want to find the best way of getting them to work in unison with one another.

The best way to do this is either by getting an integrated package in the first place, or by adding an 'integrating' environment such as Microsoft Windows to your existing software. Windows, DesQ and other 'multi-tasking' environments actually allow you to switch your work between different applications without the bother of reloading a program each time you want to use it.

Windows is probably the best-supported of these, having been written by the same people who wrote the PC's own MS-DOS computer operating systems. Windows allows you to run a number of other applications (RAM, processor-speed and disk-space permitting) alongside Windows with no special modifications.

This is made possible by what Microsoft calls a Program Interface File, or 'PIF'. It is the detail in this PIF file which tells Windows exactly how it's supposed act towards the program that you're proposing to run alongside it.

If, for example, you wanted to run a simple text-based accounting package that uses standard operating system 'calls' for printer, screen, memory and keyboard operations and required 128K, you would simply fill in a PIF 'form' using the PIFEDIT.EXE utility included with Windows. This form prompts you for basic information about how your program works (in fact, many programs already have PIF files about them included with Windows and you may not even have to specify any PIF information) and then lets you save it in PIF format.

Then when you use the on-screen pointer and mouse offered by Windows to select your existing program, it will 'know' just how to handle the program and allow it to run alongside Windows and other software.

This is made possible because Windows itself is neither entirely memory-based nor disk-based. Windows uses RAM space when it is available, but 'spools' its operations to disk when RAM is used by other co-resident software.

This approach is a far cry from the way spooling was used in the original Wordstar word-processor – which spooled everything except what it had to show on-screen – or something like Lotus Symphony, which conducts all its program operations in memory.

To use programs properly with Windows, you've got to know whether the bias of your software is towards more memory or greater disk space. On Version 1.0 of Symphony, for example, the size of your spreadsheet is limited entirely by memory. This means that in order to accommodate Symphony alongside Windows, you'll first have to shut-down all other co-resident programs (including Windows software such as Windows Write) and con-figure the Symphony 'PIF' files so that it won't try to share any services with Windows.

You'll thus be able to swap between Windows and Symphony –

but when you use any other programs at the same time, they will have to be able to run largely off disk. And if those other applications require any substantial amount of RAM, you will either be unable to run them alongside Windows, or will need to consider the addition of something like the Intel/Lotus/Microsoft Above Board Memory enhancement.

That, however, is a relatively extreme example. Most applications are nowhere near as memory-hungry as Symphony – which is, after all, an integrated package that you might not even want to run with any other applications.

With less ambitious software, a PIF set-up can be created which allows full use of Windows co-resident facilities such as data 'snap-shots' and running an existing MS-DOS application within a 'sized' window. Looking at the major parameters in a PIF file, you'll see that the first four are all pretty obvious and quite well explained in the Windows manual (see Fig. 9 below).

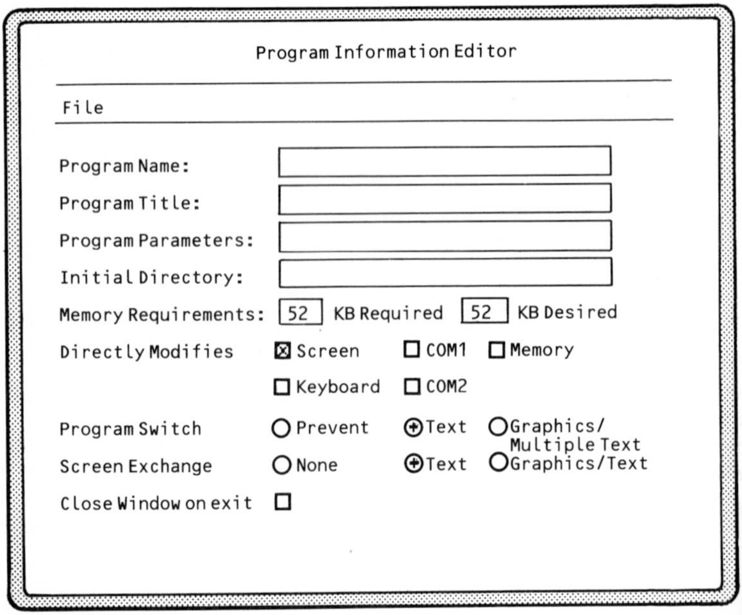

Fig 9

The first really crucial parameter you'll have to worry about is 'Memory'. Windows suggest 52K if you're not sure what it should be – but that is a necessarily simplistic estimate. Few PC applications produced in the past two years – with the notable exception of Wordstar – will actually run in 52K.

Most of the best-sellers produced in the last couple of years are slightly more memory-hungry and you would do well to check a given application's stated minimum memory before agreeing to 52K workspace.

You can, however, often get away with using slightly less memory than an application actually says it needs. Windows is designed to allow you to provide a range of memory sizes to which a given application can 'aspire'.

There is an important exception to this general method of handling things, however, in the form of applications which are entirely RAM-based. If you try to shave off a few K on such applications, you may find that you don't have enough room for any significant amount of data.

With those general guidelines in mind for determining how to deal with an application, you then need to look at which parts of your PC an application directly modifies. The first among these is the screen. If your documentation doesn't tell you whether or not it directly modifies the screen, you can check it by starting the application up in the usual way and looking at the 'character set'. If standard IBM characters are used, then it probably doesn't modify the screen – but if special graphics are employed, then you would be relatively safe in assuming that the application does.

Otherwise, give it the benefit of the doubt and try it with the screen being directly modified. You will be able to find out a good deal more detail on PIF and Windows in general through Microsoft or one of its many excellent Microsoft Press publications (I understand that at least two books have been written about Windows), but the information presented here is more of a guide to you in determining the issues you will face in using an integrating environment – whether it's Windows, Desq or TopView.

Chapter Twelve

Managing your hard disk

The MS–DOS operating system used on your PC provides a powerful 'directory' structure which allows you to organise your floppy and hard disk drives into a good number of quite distinct areas of operation.

As there isn't a good deal of room on a floppy disk (anywhere between 360K and 1.2 Mb – depending on whether you're using a PC or AT-type machine), directory organisation is primarily going to be a consideration for hard disk users – where storage sizes of 10, 20 and 30 Mb are not uncommon.

There are a number of rules which might help you in organising your hard disk data – which should follow a 'tree' structure as illustated in Fig. 10 opposite.

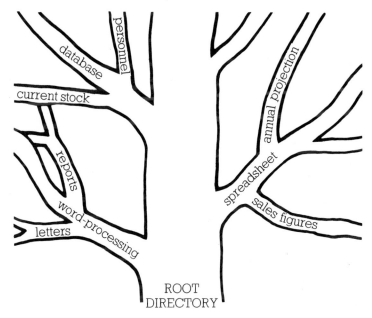

Fig. 10

As you can see, each of the major applications you have on your hard disk represents a primary 'branch' of this tree, with each off-shoot representing the people or departments doing the work undertaken in that application.

Let's say, for example, that you were using three applications on your hard disk: Lotus 1–2–3, Multimate and dBase III. To start with – at the 'top-level' of your directory – you might then have four main directories:

\SYSTEM The main system directory which will contain files for all the 'system' functions such as disk-formatting, setting the internal clock and calendar, etc.

\LOTUS This directory will contain all the main Lotus 1–2–3 PROGRAM files. There should be no user data files within the main body of this directory.

\MULTI The Multimate directory would, again, contain all Multimate's program files and the dictionary/spell-checker it uses.

\DBASE dBase III program files would live in the main DBASE directory.

Once those four main directories had been created, you would be advised to examine exactly who is to be using each of the packages and ensure that an area is cleared for each of them on the hard disk. Within the Multimate word-processing directory, for example, you might structure it like this:

\MULTI
    \SUE
    \DAVID
    \GEORGE

This would establish separate directories for users called Sue, David and George. If each of these users then ensured that each time they used the PC, they 'saved' their work onto their respective directory, the hard disk would allow different users organised access to the machine – and managers would know where to look for each employee's work.

When each user had established his or her own directory within the application, they then might further topic-specific sub-directories (ie. LETTERS, REPORTS, MEMOS, etc.) which would ensure that data specific to any given task would always be readily available in the same 'place'.

The same hard-disk organisation suggestions apply to single-users of PCs, although they would be able to omit the step of creating specific user sub-directories. A directory for each of the main applications and data-subject directories within them would suffice.

The only problem with this sort of common-sense hard disk organisation is in actually finding your way around the newly-mapped hard disk. A nice directory tree is a great help until you forget what you put in which directory. At that point you should get yourself back to the top directory with the 'CD C:\' command and and then use the TREE utility, which will list all directories and sub-directories to the screen.

The other issue to consider when using directories and sub-directories on your PC's hard disk is the difficulty of copying files between them. In many versions of DOS, the operating system will recognise files only in directories at and below the current directory level – not above it.

A good many utilities and programs which help you round this problem have been written in recent years – Microsoft Windows MS-DOS Executive and Digital Research's GEM Desktop perhaps being the best of them.

Even without this extra utility software, creative use of 'wildcard' commands should make the creation and copying of files into new subdirectories a good deal easier. If, for example, you have to do some work out of the office on a dual floppy disk machine you can ensure that you save the data created while you were on the road under a unique name – either by giving it a descriptive 'extension' or choosing sequenced names if your software doesn't allow for a change of extension.

You might thus have all the files from a trip to the US ending with the extension .USA and then doing a 'copy *.USA' to put the files onto a hard disk. But if your word-processor, for example, allowed only *.DOC extensions you could still identify unique files by calling them USTRP1.DOC, USTRP2.DOC, etc. and then doing a 'copy USTRP*.*' onto the hard disk when you arrived home.

The major thing to keep in mind when running a sub-directory structure, however, is to plan how you intend to use it beforehand. With some clear thinking and a good deal of consultation with the other people who will be using the PC along with you, you can ensure that your hard disk gives you everything you expect of it.

PART III
MAKING THE MOST OF
YOUR APPLICATIONS

Appendix A

How to buy a PC

Whether you're buying your first, second or fiftieth PC, there are certain rules which should always apply to the buying decision.

The PC you buy today is something that you're going to have to live with in the coming months and years – and choosing the wrong one could have disastrous effects on your work, the work of any colleagues who may use the machine and even the overall productivity of the firm. The good news, however, is that buying a business PC is easier today than at any other time in the past ten years.

The increasing demands of the business community have forced some sense into the traditional computer manufacturing and marketing world – rewarding those computer companies which allow for greater power and complete standardisation and punishing the ones which continually try to 'lock-in' users to unusual proprietary operating systems and non-standard hardware.

In the case of the Personal Computer, the industry hardware standard has become the Intel processor technology as used in the original IBM PC (subsequent IBM AT and PC compatibles) while the operating system and software is now based around MS/PC-DOS. This means that any machine which wants to make itself useful to the business community has – as its first order of priority – to be IBM – compatible.

Looking for a moment at the issue of IBM compatibility, it is worth exploring this issue in slightly greater depth – as many people think that IBM compatibility is simply the ability of a machine to run software written for the IBM PC. It goes a lot deeper than that.

To be truly compatible, a PC must:

● Run ALL applications software written for the IBM PC (and – where applicable – software for the XT and AT). With the possible exception of some of IBM's own diagnostic programs, it is no use buying a PC which promises to run only 'some' PC software. It means that, whenever you buy a new application, you must first test it with the machine to ensure that it will run properly.

And even when you do, there's no guarantee that sometime later – after you've already committed both money and data to the software – that some less-obvious areas of the program (such as its ability to handle certain types of printers or modems) won't 'fall over' due to the fact that your PC is only 'somewhat software compatible'. The real test for PC compatibility was established by Compaq which decided – from the first moment that it conceived the idea for a portable PC-compatible computer – that full software compatibility was essential. The company was so successful in this endeavour that almost all journals writing reviews of PC compatibles since will talk about whether or not the machine in question has 'Compaq-level compatibility'. The fact of the matter is that no other machines are as compatible with the PC standard as the Compaq offerings.

● Offer a full complement of expansion slots that are fully compatible with ALL expansion cards produced by major expansion board manufacturers. Simple software compatibility is not enough to make a true compatible. It is very often the case that popular software applications will rely on the use of certain hardware add-ons to function at their best.

Microsoft Windows, for example, will operate best with the use of its own 'bus mouse' card, many communications packages will be at optimum operation when used with an internal Hayes-compatible modem and the latest version of Lotus 1–2–3 can offer its largest spreadsheet sizes when run with the Lotus/Intel/Microsoft Above Board memory expansion board. All of these applications require the use of expansion boards to be used to advantage – and any machine which didn't allow for the use of those boards would be holding its users back from getting their money's worth out of their software.

The reasons for expansion card incompatibility are often as simple as a lack of space inside the machine. Some so-called 'clones' offer only two or three expansion card slots free – forcing you to choose which of four or five board add-ons you want in the machine (when you may well need all of them). Many others will offer the correct number of expansion slots, but may not allow the use of full-length expansion boards. Such machines (which – incidentally – include IBM's own PC Portable) limit you to the use of 'short boards' and remove much of your choice in the type, range and make of board that you can buy.

● Use an entirely standard keyboard layout. While improvements to the type of keyboard (such as providing a lighter 'feel' and a greater responsiveness) are welcome, the layout of the keyboard should not change – most software requires that certain keys are in a certain place. CTRL-key combinations, for example, are generally designed so that they work with letters on the left-hand side of the keyboard and can thus be used with one hand. If PC designers try to be 'clever' with the keyboard and move the CTRL key, add extra function keys and fiddle about with the basic keyboard layout in any significant fashion, they could add incompatibilities with a large number of applications – which rely on keys being in a certain place.

★　　★　　★　　★

Aside from these more obvious compatibility issues, there is the question of how that compatibility is used. Basic software and hardware compatibility is not that difficult to achieve these days – and many companies specialise in selling the tools for such compatibility to manufacturers.

INNOVATION WITHIN THE STANDARD

The real question is what manufacturers do with compatibility once they have it. The objective should be what Compaq likes to call 'innovation within the standard'.

This approach gets round the seemingly contradictory state of affairs which exists when you have a computer standard – yet a lot of different companies are producing a machine to match that standard. You may well wonder why – if the standard is so standard – there are real differences in the machines.

And that is where the question of innovation comes in. When Compaq talks about 'innovating within the standard', what it means it that you take PC compatibility as the first and most important issue in the design of the PC. Having achieved the best possible level of compatibility, Compaq has then gone on to see where – within the bounds of that compatibility – it can improve on the basic PC design.

ADDED VALUE

This seems a sensible approach to buying PCs as well. Instead of just looking for the minimum level of compatibility in the machines which your company purchases, you are much more likely to be looking to the long term. There is no use, for example, in getting a PC now because it happens to run Lotus 1–2–3 and then finding out when you need to use dBase III with it in a year from now that it is too slow to handle large-scale sorting in anything under a few days!

Taking the PC design as the hardware standard for your office, you will want the flexibility to 'innovate' or personalise your office system once you have mastered the basic 'horizontal' business applications we talked about earlier.

In order to have that flexibility to innovate around the PC, you must choose a PC which is going to be both powerful and flexible. And that means – coming back again to the Compaq approach – looking for a company which has performed its own innovation.

Take, for example, the company's approach to the original Compaq Portable computer. In that machine, Compaq took the basic specifications for an IBM PC and added value to it by building in a 'dual-mode' screen which would display both graphics and text on the same physical display, a composite video and RGB display interface, a parallel printer port and a unique 'shock-mounting' system around a re-inforced 'cage' to ensure that the delicate internal components of the machine were not damaged as it was moved about. All these innovations were introduced to the basic PC design without sacrificing any of the major compatibility components.

Despite the fact that it was a portable machine, the Compaq computer could use full-length PC expansion cards, ran ALL major PC applications and used a standard full-specification PC keyboard. That philosophy has come to typify the company's approach to the design of its PCs: full functionality without sacrificing compatibility and quality.

SPEED

In addition to full functionality, innovation and PC compatibility, you should also look closely at the speed of any PC you plan to buy. While PCs may look so much faster than typewriters or calculators when you first start using them, they do have speed restrictions.

If, for example, you decide to run Microsoft Windows on your basic PC system – which runs at a processor speed of 4.77 Mhz – you may find the whole thing so insufferably slow that you decide it's not worth using Windows. The truth, however, is that the basic PC is no longer fast enough to run much of the latest software which is coming on to the market.

Using a faster PC, such as the Compaq Deskpro, will get round this problem and allow you to move your software base forward along with your increasingly sophisticated requirements. The Deskpro offers a 'clock speed' of up to 7.14 Mhz and is actually two to three times faster than a typical PC in general operations. This extra speed allows it to take on more 'high-powered' jobs such as running multi-tasking programs like Windows and performing large database sorts in a shorter time.

Extra speed, however, must be used with care. A good many older applications are designed to run optimally at the slower speed and may either not run – or not run very well – on a faster processor speed. It's no good buying a PC which is simply faster than a standard PC. What you need is the kind of true speed control that the Deskpro gives you. The Deskpro allows you to switch processor speeds between the 7.14 Mhz mode and the standard 4.77 Mhz – to ensure maximum compatibility with the existing software base.

TRENDS

While compatibility, flexibility, power and speed are all important factors, there are other considerations which will impinge on the consciousness of the PC buyer in the coming months and years.

Among these will be further developments in processor technology, reductions in the size of the overall machine and the increasing sophistication and power of software for PCs. Investing in equipment which makes use of these new developments, however, should be undertaken with care and consideration. You must make sure that whatever new technology is used, however small the machine is and however fast it can go, it must still be both fully compatible and fully functional.

A case in point is the new-generation Compaq Portable II computer. Although Compaq could have used LCD screen technology, developed a machine which ran on batteries and used 3.5 inch disk drives to turn its original Portable into a laptop machine – that would have demanded sacrifices in functionality, speed and screen readability.

Instead, the company redesigned its existing mains-based machine to use the fast 80286 chip (the same as used in the AT), offer both built-in AT and PC compatibility, an internal 20 Mb hard disk, a smaller keyboard, the ability to use PC and AT expansion cards and a more compact size (meaning that the machine now sits comfortably under an airline seat and isn't so draining on the muscular resources of your arm).

Thus Compaq managed to develop a new standard for portable

PCs – without sacrificing power or functionality. The Compaq Portable II has to be the most powerful computer for its size – yet it offers all the functionality you would expect in a desktop machine.

THE 386 AND BEYOND

Just as IBM in 1985 moved the higher end of the PC market on from the 8088-based PC to the 80286 AT (closely followed by Compaq's added-value Deskpro 286), Compaq has pioneered the latest state-of-the-art PC using the Intel 80386 processor – the most powerful PC-compatible processor currently produced.

Unlike the 80286 – which didn't provide for complete processor compatibility with the 8088 used in the PC – the 80386 is fully-compatible with the 8088, but much faster.

The new machines using this chip combine all the speed and large addressable memory advantages of the AT with the software base provided by all the existing PC products. And because the 80386 is also compatible with the 80286, all existing AT software will also run on the new machine.

Thus you could quite justifiably call the Compaq Deskpro 386 – the new Compaq machine which uses this chip – one of the most powerful PC-compatible computers in the world.

Whatever name it goes under, the new Compaq Deskpro 386 has got to be the most powerful PC-compatible PC you're likely to see in the next few years. Imagine a 16 Mhz processor speed, total system memory of up to 14 Mb, hard disk capacities up to 130 Mb (with access times of less than 25 milliseconds) and an internal tape back-up system capable of storing 40 Mb.

This is clearly a machine for a rare breed of computer user and, according to Compaq itself, the Compaq Deskpro 386 is not intended for the vast majority of PC users. It's the dream machine of 'power users' and network managers – but probably offers too much horsepower for the average user.

Compaq says that it's 'setting the pace' for the PC industry with this new offering – attempting to evolutionise, not revolutionise the way users approach their data-processing work. And by keeping with the PC hardware and software standards, the company is not asking anyone to take any kind of risk.

As it always has, Compaq's Deskpro 386 is a way of innovating within the industry standard – while at the same time providing the company with an opportunity to head the market in desktop PC technology. It wants to be an industry leader, rather than IBM follower.

In fact, that company's strategy over the next twelve months is very much aimed in that direction. Compaq says it wants to maintain a lead in the high performance area, with the Deskpro 386 and 286, keep its number one position in the 'luggable' market, while at the same time developing new opportunities such as those represented by Xenix and multi-user systems.

The development of the Deskpro 386 came about partly because of market surveys which indicated there was a distinct sector of the PC market which wanted more power than the Deskpro 286 technology could provide. Those studies showed that 29 per cent of users wanted more power – and of those 29 per cent, 75 per cent wanted more speed, 68 per cent were desperate for more RAM and 65 per cent felt the need for more mass storage.

The studies also indicated a growing demand for colour displays. In recent years, colour systems have now grown to become some 40 per cent of systems sold. (A fact particularly interesting to Compaq, which had never sold a colour system).

Also projected was an increased demand for Unix/Xenix systems. Recent estimates from US analyst Future Computing suggested that shipments of Unix systems would move up from 155,500 in 1986 to 256,500 by 1990.

Perhaps the most telling statistic for Compaq, however, was the one which looked at how the market would break down between older 8088/8086-based PCs, 80286-based AT-type machines and the new 80386 machines which were under development by Compaq, IBM and others. It was estimated that by 1989 the market for PCs will be split up as one-sixth 8088/8086 PCs and XTs, two-thirds 80286 machines and one-sixth 80386 boxes.

These statistics seem to suggest that the 386 machines will largely be of interest to those 29 per cent of users who want more power – and that you may as well design a machine of maximum specification for them, and leave the bulk of the 286 market to get on with Deskpro 286s and Portable II machines. And that's what Compaq did – there are no holds barred on the Deskpro 386, it's an all-out super-powered 'muscle PC' with masses of speed and storage – without sacrificing PC compatibility.

Construction

Like all Compaq's machines, the Deskpro 386 is soldily constructed – employing the same kind of solid 'steel-cage' mounting which made the company's popular portable computers rugged enough to be taken into everything from hospitals to oil rigs.

The main CPU housing is made of a tough steel casing, which can handle the use of heavy-duty monitors sitting on top of it, while the keyboard uses the same thick and durable plastic as other Compaq Deskpro machines.

The power supply (a substantial piece of kit which is actually made at Compaq's own Texas production line, offering a peak wattage of 220) is also completely encased in its own steel housing and includes a powerful cooling fan.

Keyboard

IBM isn't the only company to have learned that people want more in a keyboard than the basic PC or AT design would allow. The first thing you'll notice is that Compaq designed its new keyboard for the Deskpro 386 with function keys (twelve of them) running along the top of the keyboard, rather than down the side – where they would unnecessarily increase the size of it.

The company also made some other changes which it may be slightly less easy for existing PC users to become accustomed to. One such decision is the movement of the CTRL, CAPS LOCK, and arrow keys. The most difficult of these to get used to (as far as I was concerned) was the CAPS LOCK being located where the 'control' key used to be. Whenever I needed to perform a function which required a control key combination, I kept finding myself in CAPS LOCK.

There are, however, also many useful additions to the keyboard. Dedicated cursor arrow keys are provided in addition to the standard cursor keys/numeric keypad at the right side of the machine, as well as a second ENTER key – with the multiply, divide, and subtract keys now located at the top of the numeric keypad.

Display

After a good deal of research Compaq determined that there was a growing demand for systems with colour display. Although Compaq's machines had always supported colour graphics in monochrome 'shades of grey' on its unique dual-mode monitors, it was clear from recent sales of both colour monitors and EGA cards that there was an interest in displays with a higher specification than that.

The new Compaq colour monitor is an exceptionally clear answer to that problem – so much so that it can be used in either EGA or CGA applications (and with either display card). In running Compaq's graphics-based demonstrations, I found the monitor to offer an unparalleled degree of depth and shading to the colours on-screen.

The Compaq colour monitor can display 16 colours at once from a 64-colour palette and offers a screen resolution of 640 by 350 pixels (for the non-technical among us, this simply means that the screen looks pretty damn good).

CPU Design and expansion

The main CPU housing is – as you might expect in a machine with this kind of specification – slightly larger than that of the other Deskpro machines and contains room for up to six expansion cards (if you're using the 40 Mb hard drive) and 14 Mb of RAM (more of which later).

There's little need to think about expansion for printers and modems – as usual with machines of this specification, both parallel and serial ports are included with the basic system (along with display adaptor and hard disk).

Buried deep inside the machine is the Intel 80386 processor, which runs at a staggering 16 Mhz (this made short work of usually-sluggish graphics environments such as Digital Research GEM and Microsoft Windows). Compaq claims the machine runs most applications a good two to three times faster than the 8 Mhz IBM AT.

The other major feature of the CPU is the fact that – like the original Deskpro – it has room for four devices, so that twin floppy drives, an internal 40 Mb tape back-up system and a 40 Mb hard disk all fit comfortably INSIDE the basic machine (although the standard Model 40 configuration will come with a single 1.2 Mb dual mode floppy disk drive and a 40 Mb hard disk).

Storage

That four-device configuration is only part of the Deskpro 386 storage story. This beast can store information – and lots of it – very quickly.

The hard disk options start at 40 Mb (with an access time of less than 30 ms) on the standard Model 40. You'll note that Compaq has quite sensibly decided that few people will want a twin-floppy machine with this kind of power and thus are not offering a twin-disk starter configuration (although two drives can be accommodated along with the hard drive).

The other hard disk system – the Model 130 – uses a massive 130 Mb hard drive (although you will have to sacrifice one of your six free slots for the more heavy-duty disk controller needed by the system) and offers an amazing access time of less than 25 milliseconds. This kind of storage has been seen on few PCs – and almost none with that kind of fast access time.

Memory

Both systems come with a minimum of 1 Mb of RAM – 640K of it currently available under DOS, with the rest available for use either under Xenix or as part of the Extended Memory defined by the Lotus-Intel-Microsoft (LIM) specification.

I mentioned earlier that the machine comes with 1 Mb of RAM and can be expanded to 14 Mb. What I didn't say, however, was that 10 Mb of that expansion occurs without using a single extra expansion slot! The other 4 Mb of RAM is provided by two 16-bit 2 Mb 'Above Board' style memory cards.

In both models of the Compaq Deskpro 386, memory is configured with standard 1 Mb of RAM actually soldered onto the memory card, so that there is less chance of chips creeping out of their sockets. The first 640K of this 1 Mb of RAM is available as base memory for user applications and a further 256K is available as standard expanded memory for use with the CEMM (Compaq Extended Memory Manager) or VDISK. The remaining 128K is reserved by Compaq for special programs designed to give users added system performance (see below for details).

In all, the extra memory in excess of 640K can be used in one of two ways:

1 As LIM specification Extended Memory – Using a simple utility called CEMM (which is included on the system disk), up to eight Megabytes of extra memory can be used in popular applications such as Microsoft Windows, Lotus Symphony, Framework II and Lotus 1–2–3. Otherwise, the CEMM works in much the same way as extended memory in any other PC (except a whole lot faster) – including 'VDISK' provisions that allow all or portions of the extended memory (a full 14 Mb, not just the eight Mb available under LIM) to be used as a 'RAM-disk'.

2 Under Xenix System V/286 – The whole of the system's memory can be used in this configuration running a multi-user PC system. Compaq recently announced support for Xenix on its 286 machines and that support will now be extended to cover the new Deskpro 386 series.

In addition, there is one further and extremely unique use of the RAM – which has more to do with the type of RAM that Compaq has employed in the machine than with the software technology which drives it. I mentioned earlier that 128K of the system's soldered base of 1 Mb RAM is reserved for special Compaq applications.

What I didn't say was that the Deskpro 386 uses two 32-bit memory expansion 'daughter-boards' on the main memory card to bring it up to the 10 Mb RAM capacity you can have without using a single extra slot. The second of these memory boards is made up of 4 Mb of socketed 1 Megabit x 1 static column RAM chips (making Compaq the first large PC manufacturer to use this RAM technology).

Because this 32-bit static column RAM is so fast, Compaq has included a utility which allows you to 'switch' the whole of the Compaq ROM BIOS into this RAM area when using the Compaq EGA card and monitor (this being the special application for which the extra 128K in the base 1 Mb of RAM has been set aside for). Memory addresses are adjusted accordingly, so that any applications you're using think that they're addressing ROM and not RAM.

The important thing about this neat ROM/RAM switching trick, however, is that it allows ROM functions to run at the full 16 Mhz clock speed when using the EGA card – and thus giving full access to the speed and power of the 80386.

Compatibility

Compaq was the company which set the standard for IBM compatibility – and it certainly hasn't abandoned that goal with this machine.

I tested it running a number of BIOS-addressable RAM-resident products, including SideKick and SideTalk, and found that it worked without fault. I also used Dbase III Plus and Symphony 1.1 (both of which can address the extra memory under the LIM extended memory specification) with the Deskpro 386.

On the latter two applications, however, did have to use the mode command (MODE SPE=AUTO) to slow down the access time on the disk drives to allow it to read properly the copy-protected applications. This presented no great problem, but I did have to remember to do it.

Compaq tells me that in ordinary circumstances I would not even have had to give the MODE command, as the machines are factory-set in the AUTO disk-reading mode – but that the test system was hardware-configured to the fastest disk-reading speed for demonstration purposes.

What all this tells me is that Compaq – while realising that it had to build a lot more power into this machine to take advantage of the fast processor, large capacity storage devices and high-speed RAM – has also built in enough flexibility to ensure full compatibility with existing hardware and software.

The Deskpro 386 will not be the PC for everyone. It is, however, arguably the most powerful PC-compatible microcomputer you can buy and certainly the fastest I've ever seen.

It will appeal to the growing numbers of corporate users who need a fast networking or Xenix solution, offer the best possible PC computing for 'power users', provide PC users with enough speed properly to run Windows, GEM and the many new desktop publishing applications which they are generating and generally present an opportunity for high-powered PC productivity.

And it certainly bodes well for the future of PC-standard computing.

Appendix B

Looking for more memory

The Personal Computer hardware standard was designed to be a flexible basis for as many applications as possible, while keeping the initial price to a minimum. This has been achieved through use of the five expansion ports, each of which can take a board with an assortment of devices attached, so expanding the capabilities of your machine.

The initial step for most PC owners is to expand the memory. If your PC is more than a couple of years old, then the chances are it contained 128K RAM when you bought it. Newer and more advanced machines may well have been supplied with 256K and if you're lucky 512K. But few, if any, will contain the full 'legal' capacity of 640K. That situation is changing quickly, however, as higher memory capacities become possible with new operating systems. As business software becomes more advanced and programs require more memory, the expansion board becomes the only means by which this advanced software can be used.

Alternatively, the more advanced expansion boards offer memory capacity above and beyond the PC limits – two or three Megabytes even, accessed using special utilities which use just some memory at a time. In this way you can have programs multitasking (i.e. more than one program running at once), so avoiding time-swapping between different applications.

The third and final use for extra memory is multitasking. This involves the connection of one or more PCs to a host computer which contains the extra memory, and perhaps a hard disk as well. Whatever use you make of the extra memory, it is an expensive item, particularly if you then have to buy the software to make use of it, but the justification comes down to the extra facilities offered by bigger programs, and their value to you.

Having decided how much memory you are going to need, use the CHKDSK Utility to check how much memory is presently in your PC. If it is less than 256K, you may be able to expand it to this figure using single chips plugged into the mother board rather than a dearer expansion board. Once you've settled on the amount of memory you will need (any advert for the software you want to run should give the memory requirements) decide how much more memory will be required and start to look round the market.

Check that each memory board you consider is actually compatible with your favourite software packages – otherwise they may stubbornly refuse to use the extra memory, or simply 'hang up'. Most major PC dealers should be able to help you here – and will have a good idea of which boards to avoid. If you want to be certain before you buy, take your software down to the dealer and make them show it running with the board you plan to buy.

When you're shopping for extra memory, note that a 'dedicated' expansion board will hold far more memory chips than a board which offers other facilities as well. The maximum RAM capacity of an IBM or true compatible is 640K, but memory boards such as the Intel Above Board can provide several Megabytes of memory.

Consider installation – dealers will sometimes offer to install the board themselves, but this can increase the cost (even if it is thinly disguised within the price of the package). Adding a memory board is usually a quite simple task – although you will have to take care that the PC's 'DIP' switches are set to recognise that extra memory.

You'll also have to be careful of simple things – leave the power on and you've wasted several hundred pounds in a flash – literally!

Once you have the board securely in the machine you will find that, like the computer itself, it is relatively maintenance free. It is important, however, to choose a board supported by your local dealer in case it needs reconfiguring. You will find that dealers will avoid boards they don't know.

Older expansion boards sometimes are 'non-standard' in this respect and should be examined with a good deal of care. Most boards produced after 1985 will largely adhere to design standards that have generally been agreed by manufacturers and should present no significant compatibility problems with popular applications packages.

There are, as we said earlier, two routes to memory expansion on most PCs – either through the aforementioned expansion board or through 'on-board' memory expansion. The latter option, which sees individual RAM chips added to the main 'motherboard' of the computer, is the preferred option because it means that you get all the advantages of extra memory without using up one of the all-important expansion slots in the machine.

If your machine does allow such an expansion on its main board, you can actually buy the RAM chips from most dealers, or from an electronic supplier, and install them yourself. RAM chips, however, are nowhere near as easy to install in a PC as expansion boards.

Expansion boards just slip into a single slot in your PC – and the most care you will have to take is in making sure the board fits snugly and that the DIP switches are set correctly. RAM chips, on the other hand, require 'socketing' small 16-legged chips into their respective spots inside the machine.

In addition to 'grounding' yourself so that your natural static electricity (which flows through any of us after doing something as simple as walking across a carpeted room) doesn't damage the chips, you have to go about the business of actually inserting the chips. To do any sort of complete memory upgrade, you will often have to insert 16 or more of these chips – ensuring that the 'legs' of each don't bend as you put them in, that all the chips are round the right way and that they are pushed firmly home.

On balance, if you do plan to install extra memory on your machine's 'motherboard' you would be well advised to get a dealer to do the job. It may cost you a little more in the short term, but the headaches it will save you in the long run will be well worth the comparatively minimal investment.

Appendix C

Banking on expansion boards

In the early days of the PC, there were no built-in facilities for using disk drives, computer monitors, or modems – but there were 'slots' into which 'expansion cards' could be plugged to provide all those things. The idea was that you didn't pay for options you didn't need and that you could customise your computer any way you wanted. Thus the world saw the rise of the first truly popular and expandable small business microcomputer.

A decade later, the expansion slot design and 'no frills' main processor board philosophy pioneered by Apple is still popular (although, ironically not on Apple's own Macintosh and Apple IIc computers) – and was taken up by IBM five years ago when it launched its now-classic PC in the United States.

The overwhelming popularity of the 'open-plan' design for computers has also given the computer industry a booming and highly-competitive business in expansion boards. There are expansion boards to provide printer interfaces, boards to add extra memory, boards which contain modems, boards which can control your household electricity – in short, boards for every occasion.

Although there are many boards still being produced for the Apple II, most of the boards – like everything else currently on the market – are for use with the IBM PC. The IBM PC – and most of its 'clone-like' competitors – come with a limited number of functions built-in and at least one add-on card often needs to be purchased to get the system to do what you want.

Unfortunately, there are only five slots inside the typical IBM PC and by the time you have the 'bare necessities' covered (one card for monitor and video output, another for the disk drive controller and yet a further one for the printer output) there isn't a lot of room for good things such as extra RAM memory, internal hard disk controllers, on-board modems, RS–232 ports, games paddle controllers, mouse input devices, high-resolution colour cards and the like.

The solution to this problem has been the invention of the ubiquitous 'multi-function board' – which is to the microcomputer hardware business what 'integrated applications' are to the software business.

A typical multi-function board will include features such as memory expansion to 640K, parallel printer port, serial interface, real-time battery-backed clock, joystick connection and 'RAM-disk' software. Some boards may also include a monochrome or colour monitor interface.

There are a number of important criteria to take into account before buying any multi-function board. The first factor to take into consideration is functionality.

Functionality is a broad criterion and addresses such issues as whether or not the expansion ports on the system use standard connectors, how large the available RAM is and what the 'bundled' software is like.

The second criterion deals with how well the board integrates with the existing IBM PC software base. There's no point in getting a board which can potentially add all kinds of extra function to your machine if your favourite software doesn't recognise those functions.

Also important is ease of use and installation. A good multi-function board should offer easy configuration of 'DIP' switches (which tell the PC which facilities are on the board and how the PC can access them) and be easily operated under conventional PC software. Trivial as it sounds, it should also fit snugly inside the PC. All too often, manufacturers can get sloppy about the sizes of their boards and you find that it's a millimetre too long or short to fit tightly in the expansion board socket.

Documentation will have a great deal to do with how much you do finally get out of the board – as different machines can require different DIP switch settings, memory addresses and I/O port configurations. If the documentation doesn't spell these out in a coherent fashion, you may have trouble even getting your machine to recognise the extra memory it's got.

The actual raw power of your expansion board will be a factor of how many functions it offers, how 'fast' it is in executing tasks such as RAMdisk operation and 'print-spooling' and its ultimate expandibility.

The first (RAMdisk) being a method of 'fooling' the PC into thinking a given area of RAM is actually a disk drive and the second (spooling) being a way of sending information that's about to be printed into an area of RAM beforehand, so that your machine can get on with other things while a document is being printed.

You should also consider value for money: how much functionality, power, documentation and ease of use you actually get per pound. Multi-function cards aren't cheap – some can cost up to half the price of your PC – but you have to weigh the price against what the cards can do.

The type of board you choose will depend a great deal on the software you want to run it with – and on the specifications of the machine you're going to put it into. Some users will simply want more memory to allow them to run certain integrated applications – such as Lotus Symphony, or Ashton-Tate's Framework – and are quite happy working within the 300K or so of workspace afforded by the 640K RAM limit of MS-DOS.

But others will either want huge amounts of space for data (and on a RAM-based program such as Symphony, extra memory is the only way to get this space) or will want to 'multi-task' (run several programs in memory at once) using software such as Microsoft Windows, Digital Research Concurrent XM, or DESQview.

On the hardware side, the specifications of your PC can have a lot to do with which card you choose. If, for example, you own a Compaq Deskpro 386 – which comes standard with parallel printer and RS–232 interfaces – then you may not want or need a multi-function board that duplicates that job.

To give you a better idea of the features to look for in an expansion board, I have provided the following brief list of definitions of those features and why they are important:

MEMORY While you won't get the Megabytes of memory offered on a dedicated memory expansion board like the Intel Above Board or the AST Ram Page, most expansion boards will offer up to an additional 384K of RAM. This extra RAM will combine with 256K of system memory on your PC's 'motherboard' to produce the 640K upper limit of RAM which MS-DOS is designed to address.

MONITOR/VIDEO OUTPUT PCs will either come equipped with monochrome or colour interface cards which allow you to use RGB and/or composite video displays. Some of the newer expansion cards – such as InterQuadram's Gold Card and Persyst's colour combo card – offer RGB colour display adaptors along with extra memory and printer interfaces. This is probably the most sensible manner in which to purchase a display adaptor if you are upgrading from monochrome to colour display. You merely remove the existing monochrome display card and replace it with the new colour card – also containing the memory and extra RAM. This means that you get RAM, printer interfacing and colour capability without using an extra slot (one slot will have been 'freed-up' by the removal of the existing monochrome card). Take care when installing a card with a colour output as it is unlikely to work without adjusting the DIP switches on the PC's motherboard first.

There are now new colour monitor standards which go beyond the existing RGB and composite video outputs. The latest is the EGA (Enhanced Graphics Adaptor) standard laid down by IBM.

At the time of writing, however, there were no multi-function boards which offered RAM and printer interfacing on the types of EGA adaptors needed to make the most of newer high-resolution graphics environments such as Microsoft Windows or Computer Aided Design software like Auto-CAD.

PRINTER OUTPUT If you don't have a printer port on your PC, there is no way you should waste one whole slot inside your PC with a printer card. Make sure that at least one of your expansion cards includes a parallel or serial printer card – with the latter being preferable as there are more parallel printers on the business market than serial printers. If your machine already has a parallel printer port, an extra port might not go amiss. If, for example, you have a need to use both daisywheel and dot matrix printers at different times during your processing, two parallel printer ports would mean that both printers could be hooked up at once. This would allow you to choose which printer you wanted to use without having to go through the business of swapping cables and moving equipment around.

SERIAL/RS232 PORTS There are always uses for more RS–232 ports. If you have one, it can be used with a serial printer or a modem. If you have two, they can be used for serial printer AND modem. With three RS–232 ports, you can enjoy the benefits of printer, modem and serial 'mouse' input device. You do, however, have to make sure that these ports don't conflict with one another. If the RS–232 port that comes with your machine, for instance, is configured as 'COM1', make sure that the serial port(s) on your expansion card aren't also set to be COM1, or you may not be able to use either.

GAMES PADDLE CONTROLLER While there is comparatively little games software for the PC, there is a space in its design for a games paddle controller (to allow the use of 'joysticks' and games paddle). This is not a feature you need actively seek out, as it still seems to be included without extra charge on most popular expansion boards.

REAL TIME CLOCK If you have ever been in a hurry to switch on your PC and cursed the convention of having to enter the time and date every time you start up the machine, then you will appreciate the beauty of the real-time clock included on many popular expansion cards. The real-time clock is actually a small crystal on the expansion card which is programmed to keep track of time in much the same way as modern watches. It even has its own battery (which you should be able to see on the board – it will be that round disk with a 'clip' holding it in place). The real-time clock need only be set once and after that the PC will be able to 'read' both the time and date from this clock every time you switch on – ensuring that your files are 'date-stamped' with the correct date and time and that you don't have to run through the rigmarole of entering it every time.

PRINTER SPOOLER This usually comes in the form of software that that comes 'bundled' with the expansion card. It will set aside part of the expansion card's extra memory as a 'shadow printer' to which a program can send all its printer information before it actually comes tapping out onto the paper. It operates by 'fooling' your software into thinking that a certain area of the extra RAM is a printer. So when your application receives the 'print' command, it sends the information off to this 'spooling' area and immediately returns the use of your PC back to you. The spooler will then handle the sending of the information to the printer and empty itself of the information once the printer has printed it.

This list of features covers most that you'll find on popular expansion cards. Many will offer extra software as a further incentive while others will make claims about the type of chip technology used and the advantages that gives. Treat the software as you would any other software purchase – and if it's worthwhile it might make the difference between one similarly-priced and featured card and another.

On the RAM-chip question, however, there really isn't too much difference between those cards that use the older 64K chip technology and those that use the new 256K RAM chips. The latter chip-set just means there will be fewer chips on the board – although they do exactly the same thing. The only real pay-off is in design. Boards which use 256K chips will have more physical room on them for other features such as video output and printer interfacing.

There is an exception, however, in the 32-bit static-column RAM chips employed by Compaq in the Deskpro 386. These allow the RAM to keep up with the machine's 16 Mhz processing speed. But you won't find them on a conventional RAM card, so unless you have a Deskpro 386 you won't yet be able to benefit from that new RAM technology.

In general, expansion cards should be purchased on the principle of 'more is better' as long as the quality and reliability of the card in question is assured. The fewer number of expansion slots you have to use to achieve the maximum power in your machine, the better.

By using a Compaq machine, you would get a bit of a head start in that department as all Compaq machines come standard with parallel printer ports, display adaptors that will work in graphics or text mode (and support colour) and memory expansion systems that allow large amounts of memory expansion on the 'motherboard' without using a single slot.

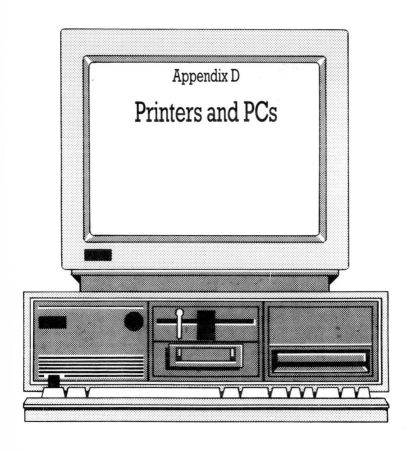

Appendix D

Printers and PCs

The reason for adding a printer to your system is obvious. Until you do, all your work and applications are restricted to the screen, which, compared with printed paper, is difficult to read, correct and manipulate. Also, your precious data must be stored on floppy disks that are not very useful to your non-PC using colleagues and far more expensive than paper.

A printer will allow letters, programs, spreadsheets, pictures, diagrams and anything else you devise on the screen to be replicated on paper, to be shown, sent, altered or stored.

Bear in mind that printers are not glorified typewriters without keyboards – their methods of printing use advanced technology of a totally different nature to most typewriters. They are designed to give a wider range of features than a typewriter, and many can reproduce graphics as well as print.

The vast selection of printers on the market can be divided into five categories – the cheapest and most popular of which is the standard dot matrix.

Dot matrix printers, as their name suggests, use a matrix of pins, usually eight wide and eight high, to print both text and graphics. These pins are fired at the paper, pressing the ribbon against it and printing the character. Different characters and graphics are simply created by firing different pins at the paper.

This enormous flexibility in the shape each character may take means a wide range of character sets may be used (as if changing the type-face on a modern typewriter) or you can design your own character sets.

Many cheaper dot matrix printers, however, do not use true descenders, (i.e. they cannot print the 'tail' on letters such as p, g and y), so the tail of those letters is moved up – which can make it difficult to read.

Dot matrix printers are, however, the quickest and cheapest method of printing available and despite their sometimes poor print quality they are also the most popular. This may be attributed to their cost and the requirements of most people to produce graphics – and not letter quality characters. The best-selling dot matrix printers are produced by Epson, which has set a standard in the lower priced dot matrix marketplace, as IBM has set the standards for most PCs.

The next step upwards in both price and quality from the standard dot matrix printer is the NLQ (Near Letter Quality) printer. Again this uses a dot matrix, and acts exactly like any other dot matrix printer. However, the print head contains a greater number of pins than normal, so producing a much clearer character image when in 'NLQ mode' by printing each character twice, the second time slightly offset from the first, so the character is darker and the dots are less visible.

Most users will find this type of printer is the best alternative, since it has all the facilities of a dot matrix printer as well as good text representation. However for the business user the quality is still not good enough in comparison with a typewriter or 'letter-perfect' printer, and NLQ mode is much slower than normal.

If you have read this far, the chances are it's because you need a printer with true letter quality. If this is not the case, take a close look at the address on the last 'free offer' to come through your letter box, and imagine sending someone a business letter of a similar quality print.

The most common type of letter quality printer is the daisywheel. This is similar to most modern typewriters, although many still use a 'golf-ball' or the old fashioned 'arms' to press characters against the ribbon. The daisywheel itself is a circular fan with a character on the end of each blade. This is held in the printer and rotated until the appropriate character is at the top, at which point a bolt strikes it from behind against the ribbon.

The quality of print is really not comparable with that of a dot matrix printer since each character is predefined. Also, while there is a wide variety of print faces available, each on a different daisywheel, these can cost in the region of £10–£20. Remember that the printer is unable to produce any sort of graphics whatsoever, and the print from a daisywheel may be slightly different to that on the screen, so it is not suitable for program listings.

When choosing a letter quality printer, bear in mind that many electronic typewriters can also be used with the PC (particularly the modern daisywheel types), so long as they have a compatible interface. Business users may find it more sensible to buy a typewriter since secretaries are usually more familiar with them than the PC, and they can be used when your PC is doing other jobs! It is also easier to type labels and forms with a typewriter since you can see where each character will be printed on the paper; and typewriters are not much more expensive than printers.

A major drawback with daisywheel printers is their speed. Most dot matrix printers can achieve 50–150 CPS (characters per second), but daisywheel printers work at 10–25 CPS, and typewriter/printers are even slower.

There is one aspect which none of the printers already covered is capable of – colour. For this luxury there are only a few printers in the lower price range, and they are of two types:

• The first is a dot matrix printer (few people require colour for text alone so there are no daisywheels) which uses a ribbon of four colours – yellow, magenta, cyan and black. These are used to produce up to seven different colours by printing one colour over another. They can also behave like a standard dot matrix printer with its various typefaces, but their small matrix means NLQ is not possible. Unfortunately, because ribbons are used, the colours are poor quality, with no brilliance, and the ribbon changing makes the printer extremely slow.

• The alternative to dot matrix for colour is the ink jet printer. Using bags of different coloured inks, this printer squirts the ink (or inks) onto the paper to give excellent colour results. It is much faster than the matrix printer, but the jets are poor at reproducing text, even in comparison with the dot matrix, so this type of printer is useless for quality reports or letters.

Ink-jet technology also has the advantage of being slightly cheaper than multi-ribbon systems, and the colours are much brighter, intense and even. This will suit the user who wants predominantly colour graphics and not text.

• Our final category of printer is not really a printer at all – but a derivation of photocopying technology. Laser printers retail in the region of £3000 and are capable of both text and graphics (not colour yet) at a standard approximately equal to the pages of your PC's type-set documentation.

Having decided the type of work or leisure for which you will use your printer, and so the type of printer to purchase, there are some points to consider as you look into various makes.

The obvious importance when choosing a printer is PC compatibility. The PC is built with no standard printer interfaces – although parallel and serial are the most common types (with the parallel or 'Centronics' interface being the most popular of the two). For graphics printing, however, the printer should be either compatible with an Epson MX or FX series machine, or with the IBM graphics printer.

While any printer with one of these interfaces will work with the PC, most software requires that each must have its own printer driver before it can be used properly. It is, therefore, worth considering printers for which drivers are already provided in your applications software – this information can usually be found in the 'install' section of your software and would typically include the following: Epson FX80, Diablo, NEC P3, Qume LP20, Smith Corona, Brother HR15, SPG 8010 and the OK Writer.

If you buy a printer for which you need to create a printer driver, check the standard of the printer's manual, which must give explicit technical details (in particular the control codes) in order to use all its features.

When you think you've found a printer you like, there are certain points you should check before committing yourself to buying it.

Firstly, there is a question of speed. Manufacturers, I assume, send several thousand volts through their printers just as they measure their CPS ratings, since these are invariably higher than the printer's true speed. The classic example of this is a dot matrix colour printer from Epson which informs you of its 160 CPS mode, but fails to tell you that in some circumstances the print speed can go as low as about 2.5 CPS! So check the speed before you buy.

Print quality is another consideration – with dot matrix printers, this depends on the number of dots in the matrix, although there is no substitute for comparing the print on paper. For graphics reproduction, check that the printer can produce high-resolution and does not rely on an extension of its own character set.

Another important consideration, particularly for business users, is the printer's carriage width. This may need to be longer than normal to accomodate spreadsheets and graphics, so check if a wide version of the printer you choose is available.

You may also require a cut sheet feeder to avoid manually entering each piece of paper, so make sure the printer has one made for it. Some printers will also take a keyboard which converts them into a typewriter which can be useful.

Also check the type of paper feed used – the two types are friction feed for single sheets or paper rolls, and pinfeed/ tractor feed, which requires special paper with perforated edges. The pinfeed mechanism should be avoided since it cannot be adjusted for different paper widths (as can the tractor feed), and it tends to screw up in more ways than one! Printers with both mechanisms are best.

Cables are expensive, and those for the PC cost far more than they should. Shop around before you buy one – after all, it's only a multi-line collection of wires with a couple of plugs on the end.

In the end buying a printer is a matter of personal choice, and available funds, but do consider what you will use the printer for before you buy.

To give a standard by which to measure low cost printers, let me give you my assessment of Epson's FX-105 dot-matrix printer. This machine has become the workhorse of the dot-matrix business computer industry and is what most other printers in its class will be compared to.

The FX-105 is one of a range of printers recently launched for 1986 (the FX-80 and FX-100 were released in April 1983). Identical in function to the new FX-85, the 105 is the largest of the new range, with an extra wide platen for spreadsheets, ledger work and pre-printed forms, where accuracy is vital.

The 105 is almost identical in appearance to its predecessor, the FX-100, but incorporates several new features. When the FX-80 and FX-100 printers were introduced, they were considerably larger than their predecessors. Ironically, Epson's latest FX range is slightly smaller than previous models – the width of the FX-105 is 59 4mm–21mm less than the FX-100, and weighs 0.1 kilos less.

The design has changed very little, except for the printer hood. This has been reshaped slightly to maximize the advantage of a new, quieter print head, which reduces the sound of the printer by three decibels. Tractor feed and friction feed are both supplied as standard.

The most important feature of the new FX range is the addition of Near Letter Quality text printing – an alternative to daisywheel print for letters and other prestigious documents. This is possible due to a new print head, which has been increased from the standard 9×9 matrix to an impressive 18×18 matrix for NLQ printing.

The printer is fashioned in cream coloured plastic, with extensive use of clear brown perspex for the cover and sheet feeder. Three buttons on the front panel are used to select on and off line, draft or NLQ print, form feed and line feed, as well as a host of other facilities, which are also software controllable.

Dot matrix printers are difficult to load with paper at the best of times, particularly when inserting single sheets into tractor feed systems. Epson started on the wrong foot with its often-frustrating pinfeed system, but the FX range now benefits from a tractor feed (adjustable pinfeed, for various paper widths) which pulls the perforated paper through the platen without it going astray.

Friction feed is used for single sheets of paper, but this requires the removal of the tractor system to prevent the sheets fouling up. It is a slow, inaccurate method of printing single pages, so Epson has developed an optional cut sheet feeder for the FX-105 (and 85), which loads the paper to the correct position automatically.

Having unpacked the printer your first step will be to set it up for the PC. This necessitates flicking a few dip switches which are conveniently located beneath a cover on top of the machine and are used to select character set, typestyle, line feeds and cut sheet feeder mode.

The dip switches also control such issues as slashed-zero characters and skip-over perforations. Many of these 'cold-start' functions are also software controllable.

The FX-105 is capable of printing at 160 Characters Per Second (CPS) in draught mode, but slows down to 32 CPS in correspondence (NLQ) mode (each character is printed twice). Proportional spacing is readily available, and can be redefined to suit your needs (if your eyesight is good enough to warrant it!)

The on-board RAM buffer has been increased from 3K to a massive 8K, part of which may be used to define 240 of your own characters. This allows you to design your own letter-heads and logos for your business and personal use. It will also store information from the PC as fast as it is sent, thereby releasing the PC for you to operate while printing continues.

The graphics capabilities of the machine are excellent – eight different graphics modes allow densities from 60 to 240 dots per inch. These graphics may also be combined with text to produce some spectacular results.

The printer gives an enormous selection of fonts – Pica, Elite and Roman, as well as enlarged, emphasised, condensed, doublestrike underline and sub/superscript modes; selected directly from the front panel or by the PC. Italics and user-defined character sets, as well as the graphics modes are also software controlled.

The FX-105 is designed to cope with paper up to 406mm wide (twice the width of an A4 sheet) so is can cope with spreadsheets, or large graphics pictures. The printer can also cope with paper as small as an address label – only 4 inches wide.

Perhaps the most important part of such a complicated printer is the manual, and Epson has put a lot of work into producing one of the best manuals on the market. It contains a comprehensive tutorial on setting up and using the printer, and provides a complex technical reference section for those experts using the printer to the full.

You can now buy a book by Collins, *Getting More From the Epson printer*, in which Susan Curran demonstrates many of the printer's features. This alone demonstrates the suitability of Epson printers for the PC. The FX printer is available with a parallel or serial interface so all of its features can be fully exploited. Included in the on-board 'DIP' switch settings is an IBM compatibility option, which makes the FX-105 'behave' like an IBM graphics printer.

The cost of the FX-105 is warranted only by its excellent features combined with a remarkable quality and reliability. At last Epson has produced a machine to rival the new dot matrix printers on the market, and the FX-105 has the power and versatility to compete with all of them.

While Epson rules the low end of the dot-matrix printer market, there may well be a number of applications for which the basic Epson product is not suited to the job. Such jobs might include plotting complex graphs, colour printing or high-speed, letter-quality work. While you may have to pay more than £1,000 for the devices to do this work properly, the increased flexibility and overall power it will add to your system may be worth it.

A good example of such a high-level printing device is the Honeywell 4/66 18-pin dot-matrix, colour, letter quality printer from Honeywell Information Systems Italia. Not only will this printer achieve printing speeds in excess of 450 characters per second and print both text and graphics in colour, but it also offers a good deal of choice in paper-handling – something which is often quite limited in less expensive models.

Honeywell spent more than two years coming up with new methods of print paper-handling and arrived with some quite unique solutions on the 4/66. For example, the printer allows you to switch automatically from single sheets to continuous stationery without having to re-thread continuous paper on to tractors in the process. When you thread a single sheet into the system (through an innovative front-loading feed system), the continuous feed paper that's already in the machine is 'rolled back' by the tractor feed motor into a 'ready' position from which it returns when you've finished printing single sheets.

If you want to print in colour, the 4/66 offers seven 'basic' colours of yellow, cyan, magenta, black, orange, green and violet – which can be combined to offer up to 27 different colours in total. Thus diagrams and Computer Aided Design/Computer Aided Manufacture (CAD/CAM) work can be shown in detail and colour, without having to use large (and even more expensive) dedicated printer/plotters.

And the 4/66 offers emulations of both the IBM colour graphics printer and Epson's JX-80 colour system – so that even if your software doesn't offer direct support for colour on the 4/66, it will be able to use the colour facilities of the printer.

In short, choosing a printer involves carefully weighing up your long-term needs against the short-term cash outlay you are going to have to make. If you only need a 'workhorse' printer which will be required to do the odd bit of correspondence and print out databases and spreadsheets, then you really need look no further than the industry-standard Epson line. But if your needs are specialised or you plan to make fuller use of the PC over time, don't be limited by the power of your printer. If you need features like speed, colour and a variety of feeding options it would probably be better to get those at the outset rather than trying to upgrade at a later date.

Appendix E

Screening your business

Having decided that 'come hell or high overdrafts' you need a new screen, the question arises 'what type, and for how much?'

There are three choices open to you. First on the list is the monochrome (single colour) monitor, which is by far the cheapest alternative. Secondly there's a small selection of 'TV/monitors' available, representing good value for money, but lacking in video picture quality. The final option is to go all the way to a colour monitor, at prices three or four times those of monochromes.

The discerning business PC owner may well have selected a PC for its comparatively low price, so a monochrome monitor is a sensible choice. Most business software PC is designed to be used with monochrome or colour monitors, and the high resolution of monochrome machines is well suited to the 80-column text mode.

The only drawback with monochrome monitors occurs when the 40-column mode (which offers a higher number of colours) is used, since colours of similar intensities are difficult to distinguish.

This mode, however, is seldom used in business and 'serious' applications programs. The screens on monochrome monitors are rarely 'black and white' and tend instead to be green or amber. Experts in screen 'ergonomics' are not entirely agreed on which monochrome screen type is best, so it's really up to you to select the one that's easiest on your eyes.

Alternatively, there are a few Monitor/TV displays on the market which accept RGB input from a video source such as the PC. Bear in mind that these are only modified television sets, so their resolution and clarity of picture does not equal that of a true monitor. These are, perhaps, the best value since a television set is included in the price – you can amuse yourself while disk drives go through a long sort of the database.

Finally, we come to the true colour monitors. These are the most popular choice for PC owners wanting to make full use of the computer's capabilities, but they are also the most expensive. Most monochrome monitors have a resolution high enough to cope with the PC and the standard PC includes at least a monochrome monitor interface, but to use a colour monitor with the PC you will need a dedicated colour card (or multi-function card with colour card compatibility).

Having decided on the type of monitor to suit you, the search begins for something suitable at the right price. There are several features you should look for when buying a monitor – the most important is the quality of picture.

Screen flicker is a recognized hazard often associated with TV/monitors, and should be carefully avoided. Anti-glare faceplates are essential – preventing unwanted reflections and reducing the screen brightness. If these two are not considered, the result will be considerable eye strain and subsequent headaches.

Anti-glare devices come in two types – either the same shape as the screen (held a few millimetres from it inside the monitor case), or as a flat piece of glass held on the front of the case. The screen should be bright (not glaring) and the contrast, or colours should be crisp and well defined.

There must be plenty of variation on the controls, which should include brightness, contrast, and image movement. This allows you to adjust the screen to suit effects created by different programs. Also, should the tube start to fade in several years, more variation of the controls will allow you to maintain a clearer picture for longer. Since the 'ON' switch is most frequently used, other controls in the front may be covered.

On the technical side, the monitor must have an RGB and/or TTL input with a bandwidth of at least 18MHz. Tube resolution varies according to manufacturers' interpretations, so the best method is a close look at the screen.

Measure the height of the screen – there's nothing worse than a monitor propped up on books so the bottom line is visible. You may not want to support a monitor on top of the PC in order to allow easy access to expansion cards. If that is the case and you do want to stand the main CPU on the floor, the screen should be tilted upwards to the face of the operator from desk level. The best answer is a monitor stand, sometimes provided with the monitor itself.

Such a stand, for example, is used on Compaq's new colour monitor – specially designed for use with the Enhanced Graphics Adaptor-compatible (EGA) display signals on the Compaq Deskpro 386. It marks a first for Compaq, after years of seeing life in shades of green and amber.

Personal preference will attract people to the shape of a monitor, but some points are worth noting. The tube tapers to a point behind the screen, so the monitor need not be box shaped.

To give you an idea of the things to look for in a monitor, I present the following assessment of two popular colour monitors: the Microvitec 'Cub' and the Sanyo colour monitor.

The Cub is an excellent monitor, completely flicker-free, and intense both in colour and clarity. Renowned for their success in the educational field with monitors for the BBC Micro, Microvitec has developed a fully compatible monitor for the PC complete with an 'all position' stand, a sloping top, and a single brightness control behind the front cover. Screen width is 14 inches (about average for monitors) and the input is RGB/TTL.

Horizontal tube resolution is 653 pixels, more than most other monitors in the same price range, and perfect for the PC's hi-res modes. Bandwidth is 18MHz, and the anti-glare CRT is built into the cabinet.

Sanyo's Colour Data Display monitor is a large and boxy affair which is almost too big to sit on top of the PC. The colours were not so light as the Cub monitor, but by comparison the Microvitec's screen was too bright. No flicker was noticeable on the Sanyo monitor and the screen was relatively easy on the eyes.

An assortment of controls appear beneath a front cover, but only two improve the screen, the brightness (when full) and the H-Center used to fit the PC picture within the screen limits. Having studied the two monitors, it became evident that shape and size were attractive, but so long as the screen was clear the picture choice was a matter of personal preference.

While that brief comparative assessment should provide you with some perspective on how to find the right monitor, the final choice will be up to you and what your eyes can live with. Take a long, hard look at any monitor you're considering and think about what it might be like if you to look at it eight hours a day.

Appendix F

More on modems

PC-based communications in the UK started as a whisper three years ago with the release of the Torch CF-500 business computer – a CP/M style business computer with built-in colour monitor, modem, RS–232 port and disk drive. Since then, the whisper has slowly grown to an audible hum as IBM stormed into the market (stamping the words 'PC-compatible' on everything that tried to compete with it) and communications products for the PC stormed in with it.

Unfortunately for UK users, most of these PC communications products have tended to be so heavily US-biased that any attempt to use UK-specific services, such as Prestel (which relies on Viewdata graphics, colour and the non-standard 1200/75 baud rate) and Telecom Gold, was either impossible, or far more difficult than it should be.

The other major impediment imposed by this US communications imperialism has been the constant references to the 'Hayes' standard for modems.

Hayes, as we noted earlier, is a US company which had the foresight to pioneer internal modems for the Apple II and IBM PC machines in the late seventies and early eighties. The company's early entry into the market (combined with a high-quality product) ensured that US software houses specialising in communications software took the Hayes modem into account when developing their packages.

As a result, almost all the US communications packages – and a number of integrated software suites – take the Hayes internal modem as the IBM PC communications hardware standard. And, if you're lucky enough to have a Hayes modem, you can auto-dial, auto-answer and even arrange 'alarm' calls using popular communications software.

Although a few other UK companies announced Hayes-compatible modems in early 1985, Hayes itself waited until late 1985 until it saw fit to develop a UK version of its modem (the company was rumoured to have been scared off by the lengthy and expensive BABT – British Approvals Board for Telecommunications – process) and thus the nicest facilities of many PC-based communications software packages were for some time unavailable to us.

Besides Hayes-compatibility, there are a number of other issues you need to address in finding the right modem for your business communications system. The first is ensuring that you have the right baud rate. The most common baud rates are:

300/300 – this is the 'slow, but reliable' baud rate used on everything from bulletin boards to electronic mail systems. It won't get your data there quickly, but you can be sure that almost any system you want to talk to will have a 300-baud 'node'. Even the Prestel system can be accessed at 300 baud – albeit without the colour and graphics for which the service is famous.

1200/1200 – a much faster baud rate which will inevitably become the main standard for electronic mail and Value Added Network (VAN) communication. And if you have large amounts of data to upload or download, the increased speed of communications will help save you telephone charges.

1200/75 – the Prestel or 'Viewdata' communications standard is very important if you want to make use of such services, but of little use if you don't. You will also find that little or none of the popular US communications software caters for this baud rate – and the special graphics characters and colours which go with it. If you plan to use Prestel – or any other Viewdata service – you make sure that you get the communications software (such as the impressive Breakout package from PC Communications) which will access it.

Many of the better modems currently offer all of these baud rates – although few of the recently-imported American offerings will support the latter 1200/75 split baud rate needed for Prestel communication. Baud rates aren't, however, the criteria on which to choose a modem.

You have also to decide where you want the modem to sit – and what type of modem you want it to be. Like most other add-ons for the PC, modems can be used internally and externally.

If you take the internal modem option, life is quite straightforward. The modem is likely to be Hayes-compatible and offer both the 1200/1200 and 300/300 communication speeds. It will also – with the notable exception of British-designed modems such as those offered by Racal and Dowty – be unlikely to support Prestel/Viewdata.

External modems come in two varieties: acoustic and 'hard-wired'. The former will require that you dial telephone numbers manually and has the advantage of being usable with almost all of the older conventional types of hand-sets, although it can suffer from background noise interfering with the 'integrity' of the data.

The hard-wired type of modem can offer all the facilities of the internal modem, such as auto-dialling and a 'clean' data line. It will also offer a greater choice of baud rates, is likely to be cheaper than an internal model and is far more likely to support the Prestel standard.

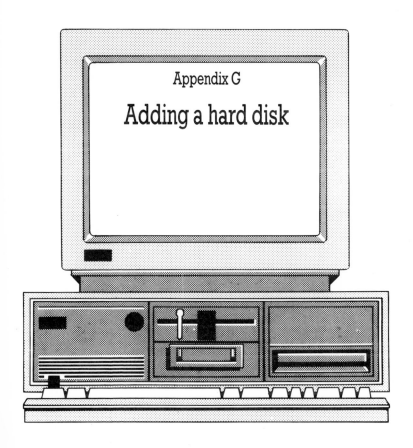

Appendix G

Adding a hard disk

The basic PC usually comes with at least two floppy disk drives and 256K of RAM – but not with the kind of large scale RAM memory or hard disk storage which is needed to run many popular applications to their best advantage.

We have already outlined your memory upgrade options – either by adding RAM chips to the computer's 'motherboard' or by multi-function/RAM boards to the PC's expansion slot. If, however, your PC doesn't have a hard disk, adding one is a slightly more difficult matter. There are essentially four ways to add 10 Mb or more of hard disk storage capacity to your PC:

- Using one of the many internal 'third-party' add-in internal hard disk upgrades, which replace the space for your second floppy disk drive. This is a simple 'XT-compatible' upgrade and represents the most straightforward method of adding hard disk capabilities. It gives your machine the same power as a standard IBM PC XT.

● Getting hold of one of the more recently-launched 'hard cards', which add internal hard disk power to your machine via a special type of expansion card installed in one of the PC's expansion slots. These hard disks on a card often don't require their own power supplies, are very simple to install and mean that you can keep the use of both floppy disk drives in addition to your hard disk. At the time of writing, the maximum capacity of such drive-cards was about 30 Mb – although that is expected to rise as the technology becomes available for it to do so.

● Adding an external hard disk system is a slightly more bulky proposition (but is less of a drain on the power supply) again means that you still have use of both internal disk drives and can also give you access to a much larger-capacity hard disk drive. External hard disk drives require the use of one slot inside the machine for a hard disk controller card and an extra mains plug for the drive.

● Buying a hard disk cartridge system. The great problem with conventional hard disk systems is that you can only back-up the hard disk onto floppy disks or a 'tape streamer' and that if the hard disk 'crashes', you can often lose all your data. Large capacity and removable hard disk cartridge systems are now available for PCs in configurations that give you up to 40 Mb or more of 'removable' storage. They require the use of at least one 'slot' inside the machine and have their own separate power supply.

The system you choose will, of course, be entirely dependent on your requirements and budget. You should, however, look for the maximum flexibility and power in the system you finally select.

The first of the hard disk expansion options – a standard 'XT upgrade' – provides you with the least attractive method of expanding. It takes up one of your disk drive spaces – limiting you to a single floppy disk – and still uses up an expansion slot as a disk drive controller if required. It is also not an upgrade you can easily carry out on your own and there is often extra cost involved in having a dealer carry it out.

If you are very keen on having an internal hard disk upgrade, the best option is something like the Mountain Drivecard – which offers a simple-to-install hard disk addition which is both fast and cost-effective. The only possible disadvantages to such an upgrade are that you don't get the security of an 'in-use' light at the front of the machine and that some drivecards may put a greater demand on the power supply which will mean that you would have to consider getting an upgraded power supply.

As long as you're not going to be moving your machine about a great deal and you have enough desk space to spare, the external variety of hard disk will probably have a great attraction. External hard disks give you the all-important access to both floppy disk drives and to storage that is measured in the tens of Megabytes.

This latter consideration is not, we should add, something that's too much of a problem in AT-specification PCs, or in PCs such as the Compaq Deskpro or any other machine that uses 'half-height' storage devices. On such machines, you can often have up to four storage devices (normally two 360K floppy disk drives, one hard disk of up to 40 Mb – or 130 Mb in the case of the Deskpro 386 – and a tape-streamer back-up).

And the cartridge external hard disk systems really do offer you the best of both worlds. They are certainly more expensive than many of the conventional hard disk sub-systems currently available, but are flexible and expandable. On hard disk cartridge systems such as the 'Bernoulli Box', you get up to 20 Mb of data on a single cartridge – offering a theoretically unlimited amount of capacity on a single hard drive (by adding new cartridges) and the ability to easily move large amounts of data from one machine to another (by taking the cartridge with you).

Further developments in high-capacity storage devices will soon see much higher-capacity hard disk drives and the release of new media. One of the most promising new media looks to be laser disk technology. There are two types: CD-ROM – based around the Compact Disc technology used in many home stereo systems and WORM (Write Once Read Many) laserdiscs. The former will only be a medium in which information can be read into the computer – but will offer up to 600 Mb on a single standard-size Compact Disc, while the latter WORM system uses a larger format of disk to offer hundreds of Megabytes of storage which can be 'written' only once.

Appendix H

PC goodies

Once you've filled up most of the slots in your machine and got a display and a printer that you're happy with, you might think there's nothing else which could possible make your use of the PC significantly easier or more efficient – but you would be wrong.

An army of new products or 'goodies' is released all the time for the PC . Probably the most prominent area of development in regard to these PC 'goodies' is the 'alternative input device'. On a standard PC, an alternative input device is anything – other than an ordinary keyboard – used to funnel information into it.

The most popular alternative input device in recent years is the 'mouse', a small plastic device (no bigger than a pair of rolled-up socks) with a wire running from it to the PC. Movement of a mouse across a flat surface causes an on-screen pointer, or the cursor to move in a corresponding manner. The mouse was first popularised on Apple's non-compatible Lisa and Macintosh PCs, but the recent proliferation of picture-based software for the PC has meant that the rodents are now one of the best-selling 'luxury' add-ons for PCs.

There are different types of mice which work with slight variations on the basic design. The simplest form of mouse – the 'mechanical' design – operates as a steel or rubber ball moves against two sets of 'rollers' inside the machine. One set of rollers controls vertical movement, the other horizontal – thus allowing movement by the steel ball (and thus the on-screen pointer) in any direction. The major drawback in using this type of mouse is that the roller can pick-up dust and dirt, thus sometimes making movement 'sticky' and jamming up the internal rollers. It does not, however, cost a great deal to produce and can be used on most flat, hard surfaces.

The other major mouse type is the 'optical' mouse. This must be used within the confines of a special rectangular pad which is a 'model' of the screen – when you move the mouse to the top left-hand corner of the pad, the pointer moves to the top left-hand corner of the screen. Movement and control with an optical mouse is often a good deal finer than a mechanical model, but it can only be used with the pad – thus limiting its appeal.

Mice also have buttons on the top side of them, to allow you to confirm on-screen selections. Although few programs use more than one button, some mice have two (such as the Microsoft Mouse) while others sport three (found on the SummaMouse).

Aside from the mouse, the other major keyboard alternative is the 'touch tablet' . It is similar in concept to the optical mouse – except that a plastic device similar to a pen is used to make contact with the pad. The movement of the pen on the pad corresponds to movement on-screen.

Touch tablets are often better for Computer-Aided Design and freehand-drawing applications, while mice are the preferred option for use in programs such as Microsoft Windows and Digital Research's GEM (Graphic Environment Management) systems.

While some look to mice and touch tablets as their relief from keyboard-phobia, others need a break from different areas of computer use. One of the complaints from many heavy users of PCs is that staring at the screen too much can cause eyestrain.

Aside from equipping yourself with an excellent monitor (see the earlier Appendix E on this subject), you can also employ anti-glare screens to your existing screen to reduce the glare and harshness of a display. Such screen shields don't cost a great deal and can improve the readability of the display.